What Others are Saying A... ...

As a cat lover who shares her life with four fabulous felines, I found a wealth of valuable information packed into an easy-to-read format. The Older Cat *should be on every cat person's bookshelf.*
—Chris Davis, *For Every Cat an Angel.*

Anyone who cares about their cat will want to keep this book in their permanent collection. Filled with heartwarming stories that remind us just how much our cats mean to our lives and valuable information and resources about how best to care for them, The Aging Cat *will give you a deeper understanding of your furry friends and help you take better care of them throughout their lives.*
—Jim Donovan
This is Your Life, Not a Dress Rehearsal

If you have a cat, you will one day need this book. The Older Cat *is filled with important questions, wisdom from those who have made critical health and life choices for their cats, and a generous list of resources to guide you along your cat's journey. You will want to tell your veterinarian, cat groomer and cat sitter about* The Older Cat.
—Andrea Reynolds (with Casper, Jasper, and Dickens). *365 Critical Questions You Need to Ask Each Other Before You Marry.*

I learned several tips that will make life easier as my two cats, now six and eight, get older!
—Sandra Williams
Williams Writing, Editing & Design.

A must-have, must-read book for every cat lover, cat guardian, and cat (of course they can read!!).
—Alan N. Canton, author, publisher, and guardian of four cats... Tekiah, Moxie, Snickers, and Pancake.

This book will help caretakers of elderly cats make the right decisions and to be comfortable with those decisions.
—Michelle T. Bernard, Boston, Massachusetts. BLAKKATZ Cattery, http://www.blakkatz.com/

Vets with a geriatric feline practice or with a growing number of elderly patients should have this book and also should encourage their cat guardians to get it. Get this book while your cat is still young; there's much here to help you make sure that your cat becomes an aged cat and that you and your feline companion enjoy many long years together.
—Pat Bell, Eden Prairie, Minnesota.
http://www.catspawpress.com/

What a useful book! I know many people with elderly cats will appreciate this wonderful resource. I am reminded of my cat, Shappho, and her last days. It was comforting to read how other people and their cats faced the same situation.
—Cate Monroe, Moon Mountain Publishing, Inc.
http://www.MoonMountainPub.com

With this book, we can make decisions to ease the pain and ease the way for our beloved companions.
—Dorothy Molstad, cat owner.

The Older Cat

Recognizing Decline & Extending Life

Dan Poynter

Second Edition

Para Publishing, Santa Barbara

Published by:
   Para Publishing
   Post Office Box 8206
   Santa Barbara, CA 93118-8206, U.S.A.
   info@ParaPublishing.com
   http://ParaPublishing.com

Printed in the United States of America

ISBN Print Edition: 1-56860-076-3
ISBN PDF Edition: 1-56860-077-1
ISBN LIT Edition: 1-56860-078-X

Library of Congress Cataloging-in-Publication Data
Poynter, Dan.
   The Older Cat: Recognizing Decline & Extending Life / Dan Poynter.
   — 2nd ed.
      p. cm.
   ISBN 1-56860-076-3 (pbk.)
   1. Cats. 2. Cats—Aging. 3. Cats—Health. 4. Veterinary Geriatrics.
   I. Title.
   SF447 .P68 2002
   636.8'089897—dc21   2001034639

Contents

About the Author

Dan Poynter is an author, book publisher and skydiver who loves animals, especially cats.

He shared his hilltop Santa Barbara home with Cricket, a black American Shorthair with bright yellow eyes, for more than 20 years. Then Cricket began a three-week decline. Dan conferred with Cricket's vet and searched unsuccessfully for a book to consult on this medical challenge. The Web contained a lot of information on cats and even on grieving but very little on the declining cat.

Being an author and a publisher, Dan knew what to do. He combined his recent experience with detailed research. Then he ran his findings past veterinarians, animal experts, nutritionists, cat lovers and life-extension specialists. This book is the result.

Dan runs his own publishing company, Para Publishing, in Santa Barbara.

Foreword

While this book is about decline, it is not negative. It will help you to recognize the early signs of winding down so that you can take measures before much organ damage occurs. Those measures may be chemical, surgical, naturopathic, a change in environment or a combination of them.

Thanks to careful health monitoring by guardians and advanced veterinary care, the lifespan of the housecat is increasing dramatically.

Your veterinarian is your partner in maintaining your cat's health and increasing its longevity. You can help your partner by closely monitoring your cat's behavior and making a written record. Early detection is the best protection against disease. Death is inevitable but it can be postponed. You are the first line of defense in fighting feline health disorders.

This book will alert you as to what to expect and aid you in making difficult decisions prior to, and after, death.

I always looked forward to seeing Dan and Cricket— they were such a wonderful team. In writing this book, Dan has given Cricket a marvelous memorial, to all our benefit. Thank you Dan, and Cricket too.

Stephen G. Lewis, D.V.M.
Airport Animal Hospital, Goleta, California.

Acknowledgment

I did not write this book alone; my friends and their cats contributed most of the material. They sent the stories, they added to the text and they even corrected my writing.

Valuable information and inspiration were contrib.- uted by Sandy Aldrich, Moira Allen, Donna Babylon, Pat Bell, Michelle T. Bernard, Robin K. Blum, Patricia Bragg, Alan Canton, Chris Davis, Jim Donovan, Beate Fisher, Jacque Foreman, Robert Goodman, Leo Grillo, Sarah Hartwell, Diane Haugen, Stephen Lewis, Pete Masterson, Dorothy Molstad, Cate Monroe, Lesley Morrison, Penny Paine, Robin Quinn, Andrea Reynolds, Dan Seidman, Karen Stevens, and Sandra Williams. Robert Howard came up with another fine cover.

I have not attempted to cite in the text all the authorities and sources consulted in the preparation of this book. To do so would require more space than is available. The list would include departments of the federal government, libraries, industrial institutions, Web sources and many individuals.

I sincerely thank all these fine people, and I know they are proud of their contributions to the cat community as well as to this work.

Dan Poynter

Dedication

For Cricket
1981 – 2001

Disclaimer

This book is designed to provide information about the subject matter covered. It is sold with the understanding that the publisher and author are not engaged in rendering legal, accounting, veterinary or other professional services. If medical or other expert assistance is required, the services of a competent professional should be sought.

It is not the purpose of this book to reprint all the information that is otherwise available to cat guardians and cat people but to complement, amplify and supplement other texts and the Web. For more information, see the many references in the Appendix.

Every effort has been made to make this book as complete and accurate as possible. However, there may be mistakes both typographical and in content. Therefore, this text should be used only as a general guide and not as the ultimate source of cat information. Furthermore, this book contains information on feline thanatology only up to the printing date.

Use caution and common sense when handling an ill cat. Clear any medication or procedure mentioned in this book with your vet before you follow it.

The purpose of this book is to educate and console. The authors and Para Publishing shall have neither liability nor responsibility to any person or entity with respect to any loss or damage caused or alleged to be caused directly or indirectly by the information contained in this book.

If you do not wish to be bound by the above, you may return this book to the publisher for a full refund.

Chapter One

Winding Down

There are more than 75 million housecats in the United States. Each year, over 4.7 million of them age, go into decline and die. Each and every day, more than 12,800 people make a difficult decision: to prolong the cat's life, to terminate it or do nothing.

Cats do not live forever. Sooner or later, they show signs of "winding down." They exercise less, they stop grooming except maybe around the mouth after meals, and they sleep more often and more deeply. Older cats eat less and may even stop eating altogether. One day it becomes apparent that the cat is declining.

The decline may be gradual and then suddenly accelerate. If your cat refuses to eat for two or three days, irreversible and irreparable organ damage begins. It is imperative that you recognize the warning signs and take action.

Once damage occurs, you must make the difficult decision: should you "play God" and put the cat down (euthanasia) or should you play nurse and make the declining cat comfortable during his or her final days?

Deciding on what to do for your aging cat is a difficult decision. And it is your decision; the cat has not signed a living will with health-care instructions. You want to make sure you are not misreading the signs of impending death and condemning a cat that could live months or years longer.

Cricket

Cricket was 18½ when he experienced a pain in one knee. He would stand and freeze because walking was painful. I wondered if he thought I was restraining or punishing him for something. My heart went out to him.

X-rays at the vet's revealed some bone degeneration. One bone was wearing while the adjoining bone had a buildup. To make matters worse, I was about to leave to run a huge conference. We expected 1200 parachute people from 35 countries. A decision had to be made. I could not carry my cat to his food to eat and to the garden for elimination—I was going out of town.

I called my friend Patricia Bragg, N.D., Ph.D., at Health Science. She is the nutritionist to many celebrities and her father started the health food movement years ago. She prescribed cod liver oil. She explained that the oil "lubricates the joints."

I bought some capsules, made a hole in one and squirted the contents onto some kitty treats. Cricket loved them. Thereafter, I made sure he received his dose of cod liver oil at least once a week.

Cricket lived another 26 months before some of his organs failed. Patricia and cod liver oil added more than 10 percent to his life. And yes, cod liver oil works for people too.
—Dan Poynter, Santa Barbara.
http://OlderCat.com

Often a change in diet or lifestyle will jumpstart your declining cat to the road back to health. Listen to your vet, your nutritionist and your cat.

Ming

"Never, never, never, never give up." This statement, first made by Sir Winston Churchill as the British troops were going into battle during World War II, is as relevant today as it was then. We can use this strategy in any area of our lives.

Recently, my wife Georgia and I had occasion to put this to the test. Our family cat (and friend) Ming had a major kidney disorder. When we brought him to the vet, we were not sure if the little guy would make it. I cannot express in words the emotional impact this had on us. Suffice it to say we were devastated at the thought of losing him. Driving home, we decided that we would not give up until Ming did.

We employed every strategy and technique we knew. In addition to what the wonderful people at the Veterinary Hospital, especially Dr. Tom Schenck, were doing to help our beloved pet, we prayed, called prayer groups and found ourselves turning to faith and developing a belief that all would be well. While we agreed that the outcome was out of our hands, we vowed not to lose faith that Ming could, in fact, survive this. I remember at one point saying to Georgia, "We're not giving up until he does."

We will never know exactly what happened but the next day Ming had improved considerably and was up, walking around the cage in the veterinary center. I believe that, in addition to what was being done medically, our unwavering belief in his ability to recover, along with the faith of the people at Edgebrook and all of the prayers being said, made the difference.

Today, several weeks later, Ming, while still not fully recovered, is back to normal. This experience has reinforced in me the belief that one should never, never give up. Whether in health matters (animals or people), business, or any area of life, it is our duty to do everything we can to affect a situation and, as Sir Winston said, "Never, never, never, never give up." Ming lived two more years.
—Jim Donovan, Doylestown, Pennsylvania.
http://www.jimdonovan.com

What does a cat sense? You know that your cat has better senses of smell and hearing than you, and many people feel they have an ability to sense danger. A cat can tell if a dog poses a threat, for example. Now you must ask yourself: If you take your cat to the vet to put her to sleep, will your trusting cat feel betrayed? Will she think it is just another unpleasant, routine vet visit? Or, will she feel it is time to go and thank you for helping?

Cats do not think that they are little people. They think that we are big cats. This influences their behavior in many ways. When we provide food, they admire us as great hunters.

Reasons people give to put down an aging cat

✔ Your cat has a terminal disease such as kidney, liver or thyroid failure. When organs fail, your cat will degenerate from toxicity and the poisoned body will die.

✔ Your cat has a terminal injury such as when your cat has been mauled by another animal or hit by a car. When everything that can be done has been done and even the most sophisticated surgical operation will not help the cat recover or its quality of life will be seriously compromised.

How we behave toward cats here below determines our status in heaven.
—Robert A. Heinlein, (1907-1988) one of the most literary and sophisticated of science-fiction writers.

✔ Your cat is suffering with pain that cannot be cured or alleviated by drugs (See chapter four). Many people feel that you have a responsibility as a cat guardian to care for your cat. If your cat is in pain, they say you should do what you can to relieve or end that pain. Causing or allowing pain is cruel. Unlike a human being, you can't explain the situation and choices to your cat.

Only the living, continue to feel the pain.

✔ You know your cat better than anyone else. Other people will rarely notice changes in eating and other behavior. If your cat cries out to you (yowls), he or she could be in pain.

✔ Your cat has become vicious, dangerous or unmanageable. As cats mature, some become irritable—sometimes due to arthritic pain. If the cat becomes a danger to children, the behavior has to be changed or the cat has to be separated from the children (re-homed).

✔ Your cat has special needs—such as diabetes (it affects one cat in 400) requiring daily treatment. Or getting weaker—and weak to the point where your cat can no longer walk so that you have to carry her to the litter box or garden.

✔ Your cat has a treatable but recurring disorders such as hairballs, urinary tract infections, ear infections, fleas, ticks, allergies, digestive challenges, irritable bowel syndrome, or arthritis.

✔ Your cat has an age-related condition that cannot be alleviated such as advanced senility, or urinary incontinence (uncontrolled urination).

✔ Quality of life. Cats age just as people do. They slow down and may become sick or injured. Your cat is to the point where she is just existing but not acting like a cat. The quality of life has degenerated.

✔ Change. The cat is not the kitten you adopted years ago; animals grow up and change. Some people get tired of their cat.

✔ Economic. Some people just cannot afford the upkeep and occasional vet bills. People who are financially challenged are quicker to make the decision to destroy. See *The Lifetime Costs of a Cat* in chapter nine.

✔ Convenience such as when the guardian moves to an apartment or senior facility where cats are not permitted.

✔ Condition of will. Some people place instructions in their will that the pet be destroyed when the guardian dies. Of course, others set aside funds to make sure the pet is taken care of.

The throwaway cat. We live in a quick-to-dispose society. When something is no longer new and useful, we often discard it. Many animal shelter workers have stories of people in the U.S. and the UK trying to trade in an older cat for a kitten.

Economics and convenience are not sufficient reason to terminate your cat. The cat has not done anything to deserve this punishment. Good vets are reluctant to destroy a cat for convenience or economic reasons. They will not put a perfectly healthy cat to sleep for the convenience of the guardian.

A cat is a 15 year-plus commitment. In return for the joy they bring, they cost time and money. People without the resources for upkeep are morally obligated not to take on the responsibility of a cat.

Abandonment. Cats are often dropped off at barns where they presumably will find mice to sustain them. Discarded cats often starve, die of disease, become "lunch" for a predator, are killed by cars or wind up as someone else's cat problem.

The more people I meet, the more I like my cats.
—Leo Grillo, D.E.L.T.A. Rescue , Acton, California.

Most housecats, though resourceful, cannot fend for themselves. Some are good hunters but others have had that instinct dulled by domestication and selective breeding. Forced to fend for themselves, abandoned cats may scavenge and eat things that will injure them. After a couple of days without food, some organs begin to fail.

Jasper

For more than a year after I moved into my home, a male orange tabby did a lot of damage trying to get in under the house and through window screens. I thought he was a feral cat, but I heard rumors he was abandoned by the previous owner of the house (who was unmistakably irresponsible in many ways). The cat, unable to get into his own home, managed to survive two severe northern winters by scavenging for food and finding shelter in garages and under porches.

Over several weeks, I left food and water for him on the deck and he ate ravenously. When I tried to touch him he cried in terror with a sound I'd never heard from a cat. Eventually he came into the house and spent up to 8 hours at a time just sleeping. It was obvious this had been his home.

I already had two cats and really couldn't afford a third, nor was I willing to risk whatever disease, like feline leukemia, he could bring to my healthy cats. But he looked underweight and undernourished and I couldn't bear to let him deteriorate.

I scooped him up, took him to the nearest vet and discovered he was full of parasites and very near death. Our veterinarian is certain this cat was terribly abused. I brought him home and isolated him for 2 weeks.

The very next day my neighbor appeared at my door asking if I had her cat. She couldn't describe his markings and even volunteered she thought he was dead. I said it couldn't be her cat if she couldn't describe it, and being a nurse as she was in the healing professions, she couldn't possibly have allowed a living creature to become so desperately ill.

An hour later the police were at my door; she'd accused me of stealing her cat. When the policewoman saw the condition of the cat and the two-page vet bill, she just rolled her eyes and left.

A year later Jasper is a healthy affectionate cat, purrs as loud as a lawn mower, but still flinches in fear of any quick movement.
—Andrea Reynolds, Lake City, Pennsylvania.
http://www.AndreaReynolds.com

Your belief system. Some people believe that life is sacred and do not wish to take a life—any life. They treat animal life as they do human life and let the cat die a natural death. Others believe that animal life has little value, so when the cat becomes inconvenient, they eliminate the inconvenience.

Many people fall somewhere in between but rank human life above animal life. For example:

And God said, Let us make man in our image, after our likeness: and let them have dominion over the fish of the sea, and over the fowl of the air, and over the cattle, and over all the earth, and over every creeping thing that creepeth upon the earth.
— Genesis 1:26.

The Book of Genesis says that God gave man stewardship over the animals. With that privilege came the responsibility of caring for the animals properly. God may be trusting you to make the correct decision.

While you have the power of life and death over your pets, you also have the authority to decide the type of death. A quick and humane end may be preferable to both your household and the cat than a lingering, suffering end.

By medicine life may be prolonged, yet death will seize the doctor too.
— William Shakespeare (1554-1616)
English poet, dramatist and actor.

Drawing the line. Having the power of life and death is a great responsibility. How far do you want to go? Where do you want to draw the line?

- Destroy the cat at the first sign of decline.
- Withhold medical treatment
- Relieve pain but let Nature take her course.
- Hydration, medication, force feeding.
- Life support such as intravenous feeding for nutrition and hydration. Utilize every means to keep the cat alive as long as possible regardless of the cat's ability to function or the expense.

The decision. So you have a big decision to make: Do you plan to play God by taking your cat to Doctor Katvorkian? Or, will you play Florence Nightingale and make your cat comfortable during his or her final days? You must estimate and weigh the cat's chances for recovery, potential disabilities and long-term medical challenges.

These next few chapters will tell you what to expect whatever your choice.

The Cat's Prayer

Anonymous

Although I am too proud to beg, and may appear to be a very independent creature, I ask for your loving care and attention. I rely on you for my well being much more than you may realize.

This I promise you, my benefactor, that I will not be a burden on you nor will I demand more of you than you care to give.

I will be a quiet peaceful island of serenity for you to gaze upon; a soft soothing body to caress, and I shall purr with pleasure to rest your weary ears.

Since I am a gourmet who appreciates different taste sensations, I pray you will give me a variety of nutritious foods and fresh water daily.

You know dear friend, how I love to go. Allow me, I pray, a warm sheltered place where I can rest peacefully and feel secure.

If I am wounded in battle or suffering from disease, please tend me gently, and see that loving and competent hands treat me.

Please protect me from the inhuman humans who would hurt and torture me for their own amusement. I am accustomed to your gentle touch and am neither always suspicious nor swift enough to avoid such malicious acts.

In my later years when my senses fail me and my infirmities become too great to bear, allow me the comfort and dignity that I desire for my closing days and help me gently in my pain or passing.

Hear this prayer, my dear friend, my fate depends on you.

Chapter Two

The Ages of Cats

In 1987, cats overtook dogs as the number one pet in the United States. Today, there are approximately 75,076,000 cats in the U.S. Three in ten (or 35,459,000) U.S. households have at least one cat. Half of those households have one cat; the rest of the homes are shared by two or more cats.

For additional pet guardianship statistics, contact the American Pet Products Manufacturers Association: http://www.appma.org

Age is a matter of feeling, not of years.
—George William Curtis (1824-1892)
Writer

Cat year conversions

First six months = 10 cat years, a kitten.
Second six months = 5 cat years, a teenager.
Each year thereafter = 4 cat years, a mature adult.

For an online cat age calculator, see
http://www.blakjak.demon.co.uk/cat_yrs.htm

Cat life stages

Birth to 16 weeks
Your kitten is just learning her way around. She may be playful but will most likely be shy. This is a small cat in a big new world.

16 weeks to 1 year
Your kitten will become very playful and adventuresome. Prior to six months of age, it is time to spay or neuter your cat. Neutering a cat extends its lifespan by two or three years; they become healthier and easier to live with.

1 to 8 years
Your young cat is in his prime. His personality will emerge.

8 to 12 years
Your middle-aged cat may begin to slow down, but her behavior should not change very much. Be alert for kidney failure, liver failure, diabetes and dental health. Think about preventative medicine. Have her blood checked annually. Your vet may recommend a change in diet and some nutritional supplements.

12 to 15+ years
Your cat is entering old age. He or she may move more deliberately, sleep more than 18 hours each day and may become easily irritated. Monitor your

cat regularly for health changes and log them in a journal.

Cats sleep anywhere, any table, any chair.
Top of piano, window-ledge, in the middle, on the edge.
Open drawer, empty shoe, Anybody's lap will do,
Fitted in a cardboard box, in the cupboard with your frocks—
Anywhere!
They don't care!
Cats sleep anywhere.

—Eleanor Farjeon (1881-1965)
English writer for children.

Life expectancy is increasing. With cat care education, neutering, vaccination programs and improved veterinary care, cats are living longer. Today, they spend more time in their middle-aged and senior stages. Some people say that today middle age begins at 10 and old age at 15.

Aging seems to be the only available way to live a long life.
—Daniel Francois Esprit Auber (1782-1871)
French Composer.

The average lifespan of an outdoor-only cat (feral and non-feral) is about 3 years; the average life expectancy for a neutered, well-looked-after cat is now 15-17 years for a male and 17-19 years for a female. Cats, like people, are living longer. The oldest recorded age for a cat is 34 years. In 1930, cats averaged just 8 years.

Housecats allowed access to the outdoors will get more exercise and are less likely to become bored or lonely. But the outdoor cat will be exposed to feline diseases from the other cats she encounters. Then, there are bobcats (yes, they eat housecats), coyotes, hawks and other predators. If you live in town, cars pose a constant threat. The dangers depend on your locality and whether you have a fenced, outdoor run. Free-roaming outdoor housecats average eight years.

**If only, when one heard that old age was coming, one could bolt the door, answer "Not at home" and refuse to meet him.
—Kokinshu, 905 C.E.
Japanese poet**

Siamese (short-hair) cats seem to live longer while Persians (longer hair) have shorter life spans.

It has been said, "cats have nine lives." Cats were given nine lives because they were considered lucky. Back then the number 9 was very lucky because it was the "trinity of trinities."

If we divide the 75 million housecats by 16 years, we find that 4.7 million are reaching old age and dying each and every year. In many cases, they go into decline and their guardian has to make a decision. In addition, 5 million or more unwanted cats and dogs are destroyed at animal shelters annually.

The decline. Because your cat is constantly with you, you probably will not notice the subtle, evolutionary changes taking over her body. You may observe a reduction in energy and that the cat no longer jumps up to high places. Then you may notice changes in eating habits, health and overall behavior. If your cat has continual access to dry food, you may not notice that she is skipping meals—until there is significant weight loss.

**Growing old is like being increasingly penalized for a crime
you haven't committed.**
—Anthony Powell (1905-2000)
English novelist

Predictions. Some illnesses progress slowly while
others are more rapid. Cats are good at hiding the
signs of illness; they may reach advanced stages of
organ deterioration before you notice.

**My vets have always told me that anything over 12 is a gift.
Your cat lived to 20—you have been gifted, indeed.
—Jacque Foreman, Altadena, California.**
http://www.abacus-es.com/foreman

Your vet probably will not be able to predict life
expectancy, but may give you some general
guidelines. The type of illness, its progression, the
cat's age and general condition will all play a part in
the vet's calculation. The vet may opt for a complete
physical exam including blood, urine, stool, biopsies
and x-rays or scans to determine and quantitatively
measure the progression of the illness.

A cat that refuses all food may last two weeks or
more, depending on the amount of stored body fat.
But the cat may have been losing weight for some
time. A cat that refuses water may last only a few
days.

Watch your aging cat for any changes in behavior.

If I Should Grow Frail

Anonymous

If it should be that I grow frail and weak
and pain does keep me from my sleep,
then will you do what must be done
for this—the last battle—can't be won.

You will be sad; I understand
but don't let grief then stay your hand.
For on this day, more than the rest
your love and friendship must stand the test.

We have had so many happy years;
you wouldn't want me to suffer so.
When the time comes, please let me go.

Take me to where my needs they'll tend,
only, stay with me until the end.
And hold me firm and speak to me
until my eyes no longer see.

I know in time you will agree
it is a kindness you do for me.
Although my tail its last has waved,
from pain and suffering I have been saved.

Don't grieve that it must now be you
who has to decide this thing to do.
We've been so close—we two—these years,
don't let your heart hold any tears.

Chapter Three

Making an Educated Decision

The more you find out about your cat's illness or condition, the more informed your decisions will be. Here are the tough questions to research, put to your vet, share with family members and ask yourself.

✔ How much do I know about my cat's condition?

✔ Are there any new or *experimental* treatments available for this condition? What are the alternatives?

✔ Are there any new *surgical* techniques for this condition? Are they experimental?

✔ Is my cat in great pain, distress or mild discomfort? Can the pain be realistically alleviated to give the cat a reasonable quality of life for a period of time? If so, for how long?

✔ Is my cat eating regularly?

✔ Is she playful and affectionate? Or is she tired and withdrawn?

✔ Should I get a second opinion from a vet who specializes in cats? Another doctor may have different experiences or new information.

✔ How much will each type of treatment cost? Can I afford the treatment?

🖋 Can I administer treatment at home? Am I prepared to give daily tablets, daily injections feed a prescription diet or carry the cat to the litter box?

🖋 Will the cat physically resist treatment? Will treatment require two people?

🖋 Will the treatment or side-effects cause distress for either of us? Am I up to administering treatment?

🖋 Will traveling for treatment or surgery distress my cat?

🖋 Do my other cats risk being infected by the disease or can they be inoculated? Can I keep the cat separated from the other cats?

🖋 How fast does this illness progress and what are the signs of its progression?

🖋 How fast will my cat deteriorate with and without treatment? Compare.

🖋 What sort of life expectancy does my cat have with and without treatment?

🖋 Will treatment prolong my cat's life or merely prolong suffering? Is this disorder curable?

Ask your vet to describe your cat's condition in terms you can understand. If you write down your questions before your visit, there won't be any you forget to ask.

Get your vet's email address so you can keep him or her posted on your cat's progress. If your vet notices something going wrong, he or she may suggest a visit. Do not overdo this service; don't be a pest. Keep your vet posted but do not ask questions that require a reply unless absolutely necessary. Save questions for the visits.

What is good for the goose. One way to decide on what to do is to consult your own will or living trust. What *Advance Health Care Directives* have you selected for yourself? Obviously you thought about how you wish to be treated if you are incapacitated and can't voice your wishes. You wrote them down and signed them before a notary public.

Did you decide on life support to keep you alive at all cost or did you instruct the caregivers to pull the plug? When you stop eating (maybe because of unconsciousness) do you want to be fed intravenously? If you made these decisions for yourself, you may wish to you treat your declining cat the same way.

Your own health care instructions may read as follows:

☐   I want to die a natural death without having my life prolonged by machines or non-beneficial treatment.
☐   I want to die free of unnecessary pain and suffering even if pain medication will shorten my life.
☐   I don't want my life prolonged by any means when this life has no more meaning for me.
☐   Regardless of my condition, it is my desire to receive nutrition and hydration in all ways possible.
☐   Regarding the decision to withhold or withdraw life-sustaining treatment, I desire my agent to act after allowing a reasonable period of time for observation and diagnosis.

Quality of life. Cats are concerned about the quality of life, not the length of life. They are concerned for the moment and their next meal, not about lasting until the holiday season. To a cat, a shorter fun life is preferable to a longer miserable one.

Operations, on humans and cats, may save a life but also pose certain risks from the anesthetic and trauma. The risks increase as the cat ages.

Some remedies are worse than the disease.
—Publilius Syrus (**circa 45 B.C.E.**)
Roman author

Consider the side effects of treatment—from daily shots to weekly dialysis for kidney failure. What will be the effect of administering general anesthetics repeatedly? What if the cat doesn't respond to treatments or the body reacts and begins shutting down? The treatment may be worse than the illness.

If your cat is weak, it may be necessary to feed a special food for a few weeks to build up her strength. If her condition requires the operation sooner, there may not be time to prepare for the procedure.

Many decisions have been made for your cat: neutering, declawing, type of food and so on. Now you are charged with the ultimate decision. Each cat and each situation is different. Many cat guardians are most concerned about pain. If the pain cannot be reasonably relieved, they feel justified with putting the aging cat away.

If it is any comfort, remember that in the wild, other animals eat animals long before they get this far. Death is a natural cycle of life.

When you look back on your decision, will you feel you betrayed the trust your cat had in you or will you wish you made the decision sooner?

Search the Internet for information. Some URLs are listed here. Print out interesting, relevant pages and discuss your findings with your vet. Remember that all medical treatments and procedures are not available in all areas.

Once you get enough good information, you can make an informed decision for your precious cat.

There is a New Star Shining in the Sky Tonight ...

There is an old belief that the stars shining in the night sky are the spirits of those who have died. They have shed their earthly bodies and exchanged them for bodies made of light; thousands upon thousands of our dear departed friends all promoted to glory in the night sky. There is another saying that the brightest flame burns the shortest.

My friend, you were the brightest star in my own universe. While I burn on, my flame dimmed by grief and despair at your passing, the stars are watching me. They are too far away for me to touch, just as you have gone somewhere I cannot follow until my own star-time comes. They cannot be held close for comfort, just as I can no longer hold you close, though I held you close to comfort you in your final hours. We were together for such a short time, but the stars will burn forever.

One day I will grow tired of this earthbound body, my own star-time will come and my spirit will soar into the sky to burn with all those friends who have gone before me. On the inky cloth of space we will be reunited in constellations of joy. Until then, my flame burns low and dim and cold without you. Through my tears I look upwards to see if you are watching me and what do I see?

There is a new star shining in the sky tonight.

Chapter Four

Signs of Decline

As your cat grows older, there will be changes in both physical condition and behavior. As the systems of the body slow down, joints will stiffen and some of the senses will not be as sharp.

Eventually, every cat goes into decline unless she meets with an accident or a predator. The old or terminally ill cat begins to deteriorate. The more common disorders are kidney disease, heart disease, diabetes, thyroid problems and cancer. The progress of some diseases can be slowed if they are caught early enough. Unless you weigh your cat regularly and keep notes on her behavior, you may not notice the decline at first. For a more detailed list of signs and symptoms, see the *Cat Owner's Home Veterinary Handbook* by Carlson and Giffin. See the Appendix.

As cats mature, they recover more slowly from illness and injury.

The aging of your cat will be affected by heredity and environment. Good genes are a matter of luck, but there are a number of ways to alter the environment, to slow the age clock, including nutrition and health care.

A physician can sometimes parry the scythe of death, but has no power over the sand in the hourglass.
—Hester Piozzi Thrale (1740-1821)
English writer

As many as 50 percent of today's cat guardians never take their cats to a veterinarian for health care. And since cats tend to hide their health challenges, many guardians think their cat is perfectly healthy when actually he or she may be suffering from a life-threatening disease. Therefore, cats tend to be much sicker than dogs by the time they are brought to the vet for treatment.

When you do notice that the cat is "different," it may be due to a treatable illness or the cat may be in a terminal decline. You may be able to save the cat or at least extend his or her life through simple and inexpensive means, especially if you recognize the symptoms of decline early enough.

Most people think that aging is irreversible and we know that there are mechanisms even in the human machinery that allow for the reversal of aging, through correction of diet, through anti-oxidants, through removal of toxins from the body, through exercise, through yoga and breathing techniques, and through meditation.
—Deepak Chopra, author of 25 books
on the balanced integration of body, mind and spirit.

Common symptoms in aging cats and possible causes.

Most cats approaching death display at least one of the following symptoms. See the explanations that follow in this chapter.

- Weight loss
  Metabolic disorders: thyroid, liver, kidney; parasites; or just getting more exercise.
- Appetite loss
  Dental disorders; liver disease; kidney disorders; viral or bacterial infection; tumor; or just eating out.
- Eats more but does not gain weight
  Hyperthyroidism; early diabetes; parasites; getting more exercise.
- Drinks more water or more frequently
  Hyperthyroidism; diabetes; kidney disease; or eating dry food.
- Chewing difficulties, bleeding gums, bad breath.
  Diseased teeth; gum disease; mouth tumor; foreign body.
- Mouth odors
  Sweet smell may indicate kidney disorder.
  Rotting smell may be due to a dental disorder or cancer.
- Vomiting
  Hairballs; poisoning; viral infection; parasites; foreign body ingested; irritable bowel disease; carsickness; eating too quickly.
- Constipation
  Hairballs; poor diet such as too much dry food; intestinal tumor; colon problems.
- Increased urination
  Diabetes; kidney degeneration; drank too much water.
- Difficulty urinating or misses the litter box when urinating.
  Kidney disorder; Feline Urinary Syndrome (FUS).
- Diarrhea

Liver disease; parasites; irritable bowel disease; spoiled food; ate too quickly; can't digest milk.

- Frequent colds, infections and illness.
  Impaired immune system; feline leukemia.
- Uncontrollable salivation
  Dental disorder, something stuck in throat; rabies; poisoning; carsickness.
- Skin problems, severe itching, diarrhea, vomiting.
  Food allergies; fleas; ringworm; liver disease, or chemical sensitivity.
- Lumps under the skin
  Tumor; cysts; cancer.
- Behavioral changes: pacing the floor, acts differently.
  A sociable cat that suddenly wants to be left alone or an unsociable one that constantly seeks reassurance may be trying to tell you that he is unwell.
- Hyperactivity along with thirst, diarrhea and weight loss.
  Check for hyperthyroidism.
- Yowling/loud crying.
  Failing senses such as eyesight. Hyperthyroidism. Degeneration changes to the central nervous system.
- Limping, stiff after naps.
  Arthritis, kidney failure.

Yowling. Some cat experts feel that cats become anxious and yowl as their sight and hearing deteriorate. Night-time yowling usually occurs when the nocturnal animal is most active: during dusk and dawn. Many geriatric cats yowl at night but some may yowl at any time.

Some older cats are simply seeking company and reassurance. You might try letting her sleep in the bedroom, near you.

Your cat may be suffering from cognitive disorders from decreased mental ability such as confusion and loss of orientation. Or, the yowling may indicate high blood pressure (hypertension). Hypertension is normally associated with kidney failure.

Cats are rather delicate creatures and they are subject to a good many different ailments, but I have never heard of one who suffered from insomnia.
—Joseph Wood Krutch (1893-1970)
American naturalist, conservationist, writer, and critic.

If your cat has been yowling, blood pressure medication to lower the pressure may quiet her. Your vet will check for hyperthyroidism and hypertension and may prescribe an antihistamine. Some cats respond to anti-anxiety medications. Vitamin B is a good stress reducer for cats.

Pain. Your cat may tremble, shiver or shake when he is in extreme pain. You may be terribly distressed because you can't ask what hurts and can't explain what you plan to do to relieve the pain.

Purring does not necessarily indicate your cat is happy and healthy. Cats may purr at other times: when in pain, when scared, and even when asleep.

Do not give your cat commonly used arthritis drugs designed for humans such as aspirin, acetaminophen, or ibuprofen. They are lethal to cats.

Sleeping. Mature cats with no health problems are in deep sleep 15 percent of their lives. They are in light sleep 50 percent of the time. That leaves just 35 percent awake time, or roughly 6-8 hours a day. Expect your older cat to sleep 18 hours each day. Cats come back to full alertness faster than any other creature.

Cricket just turned twenty but he slept through at least 19 of those years. He thinks he is only one—at least that is all he can remember.
—Dan Poynter
http://OlderCat.com

Mood. You can tell a cat's mood by looking into her eyes. A frightened or excited cat will have large, round pupils. An angry cat will have narrow pupils. The pupil size is related as much to the cat's emotions as to the degree of light.

The domestic cat is the only species able to hold its tail vertically while walking. You can learn a lot about your cat's present state of mind by observing the posture of her tail.

Skin and coat changes indicate something is going on. The only place the hair should be thin is between the eyes and ears. If the cat's coat becomes dull, dry,

oily or unkempt, the cat is most likely not well. Look
for a decrease in grooming, looser and drier skin and
lumps and bumps.

Grooming. A cat will spend a
good portion of her life washing
herself. Longhaired cats have
even more work to do and will
benefit from human help. Both
long- and short-haired cats have
about the same number of hairs
(130,000 per square inch on the

belly) but the longer hairs are more visible. Older
cats may stop grooming except after meals and then
only around the mouth. This happens as they feel
the arthritic affects of advancing age and become
less supple.

Cats aren't clean; they're covered with cat spit.
— John S. Nichols (1745-1846)
English writer and printer.

Thinning haircoat and dry skin may be treated with
a fatty acid supplement.

Check around the back end. Longhaired cats may
have some feces hanging on under the tail. Older
cats find it more difficult to bend enough to get back
there to clean it up. You may use blunt-pointed
scissors to trim some of the hair in this area.

You can keep your cat clean, healthy and sweet
smelling through brushing and combing.

It is with the approach of winter that cats...wear their richest fur and assume an air of sumptuous and delightful opulence.
—Pierre Loti (1850-1923)
French naval officer and novelist.

Your choice of brush or comb will probably depend on hair length. The cat may like brushing better as there is less pulling on the coat. Either one will remove loose hair, which will reduce shedding and prevent matted fur. Removing excess hair will reduce its ingestion by the cat and the resulting fur balls.

His tongue is a sponge, and brush, and towel, and currycomb. Well he knows what work it can be made to do,
Poor little washrag, smaller than my thumb.
His nose touches his back, touches his hind paws too. Every patch of fur is raked, and scraped, and smoothed.
—Hippolyte Taine (1828-1893)
French thinker, critic, and historian.

Your cat will probably like having his back brushed or combed and dislike your stroking his chest and abdomen.

Front legs bowed or "Clockwork Kitty Syndrome." One day you may notice your cat's front legs appear to bow outwards. His or her body may be sagging and the cat is spreading the legs apart to admit more air into the lungs.

Back legs bowed. Older cats have a tendency to walk on their hocks due to muscle deterioration in the hind legs and haunches. You may note that your cat is not jumping as high—on to counters or up on fences. Your cat may have saddle thrombus—a clogging of the arteries serving the hind legs. This disorder reduces the blood flow to the hind legs causing muscle deterioration.

The sense of smell and the sense of taste. Cats have a special scent organ located in the roof of their mouth, called the Jacobson's organ. This organ analyzes smells and is the reason why you will sometimes see your cat "sneer" when he encounters a strong odor. This is an olfactory reflex.

There is no snooze button on a cat that wants breakfast.
—Unknown

Stomach disorders may result in Lake of appetite, weight loss, vomiting or diarrhea.

Loss of appetite (anorexia). Just like people, cats need to eat when they are sick. Also, just like people, they often lose interest in food at this time. The main difference between the two is that you can try to reason with people.

Cats can suffer liver damage from not eating for two or three days. When the stomach is empty, the body uses its fat stores for fuel. Unfortunately cats are not very good at using stored fat for energy, and thus the fat can begin to accumulate in the liver. Next, the body burns muscle to keep the heart pumping and the lungs breathing. The result may be weight loss, diarrhea, anemia, and a general wasting away. Irreversible and irreparable damage is taking place.

If your cat refuses food, here are a few things you can try to stimulate a renewed interest in eating:

🐾 Hand feeding. Your cat may respond to the special attention. But you may find that after a few tiny morsels, the cat's (shrunken) stomach is full and further offerings are refused.

Paprika

Paprika had a tumor in her chest making it hard for her to breath. When she came home from the vet's office, she was definitely picky about what she would eat, if she would eat at all. It was necessary to take her back on a regular basis to get the fluid drained from her chest cavity. Eventually she decided not to eat. She would drink water.

Because Paprika was on some pretty powerful medication, she would vomit up straight baby food meat. A client of mine who had nursed several sick puppies suggested that I mix the baby food meat with tofu because tofu is high in protein, but easier to digest. I used the firmest tofu, and mixed it about 1:1 by volume with the baby meat. This mixture retains its "stickiness," so it sticks to the roof of her mouth.

I experimented with the best procedure for feeding her. We (Paprika and I) decided that the best thing to do was to put her in one of the plastic scoop chairs in the kitchen. I leaned over the back of the chair, opened her mouth, and put a fingerful of food on the roof of her mouth. She "tongued" it off, and I gave her another. She had to get the equivalent of 5 fingersful down for each meal. After feeding her, she got a big hug. She lasted another six or eight months.
—Jacque Foreman, Altadena, California.
http://www.abacus-es.com/foreman

🐾 Feeding special treats such as chicken, turkey or fish.

I can resist everything except temptation.
—Oscar Wilde (1854-1900)
Irish wit, poet and dramatist.

✔ Warm the food in the microwave to increase the aroma and make it more attractive to the cat. Touch the food with a finger to make sure it is not hot. Often the aging cat's teeth have become sensitive to cold food.

✔ Use a stronger-smelling food. Try mixing in some juice from canned fish. Dry kibble has less odor than canned or moistened foods.

✔ Force feed baby-food meat and vitamins with a syringe.

A cat cannot see directly under his nose. This is why she cannot seem to find tidbits on the floor. Cats can't see food that does not move. That is why (slower-running) rabbits freeze. Cats find their food by smell.

You can puree the cat's food in a blender and squirt small amounts into her mouth with a syringe or turkey baster (if she has a large mouth). Force feeding should only be tried when the cat refuses all food on her own. Check your vet and pet stores for liquid cat foods.

Your vet may prescribe Milk Thistle, Diazepam (Valium), Oxazepam (Serax), Periactin, and/or Flurazepam (Dalmane) to jumpstart the appetite. Milk Thistle is especially useful when there are liver problems as it also has some beneficial properties for the liver. Your vet may also treat an underlying cause.

Your vet can also insert a tube into the cat's stomach for feeding, if needed. In cases where it is necessary for the cat to eat to reverse medical problems, such as hepatic lipidosis, this may be the only way to force the cat to get the amount of nourishment she needs.

Weight loss may not be immediately visible, especially if the cat is overweight and has a thick coat.

According to Purina's *State of the American Pet Survey*, 76 percent of cat guardians do not believe their cat has a weight problem.

Cachexia is a weight loss condition occurring in animals with advanced illness; it poses challenges for both vets and loved ones. Now the cat is weak and is not interested in eating; he or she is slowly wasting away.

Your vet will probably recommend a high-protein, high-energy diet and a multivitamin/mineral supplement. Two brands of high-calorie, high energy, food supplements are Nutri-Cal® and Vitacal®.

Weigh your cat every two months; weekly if he or she appears to be in decline; daily if sick. Fluctuations of three pounds over a three-month period are a danger signal.

Your cat's weight will vary from hour to hour depending upon food and water intake and their elimination. Do not be alarmed by a small change; look for trends. But if your cat drops from 12 lbs. to 11.4 lbs. in a week, that is a drop of five percent. If you weigh 160 lbs., that would be like losing 8 lbs. in seven days.

Most bathroom scales are not accurate in the lower range. Buy a better scale. Or ask your vet if you may bring your cat in periodically for a free weigh-in.

Vomiting or "throwing up" is the involuntary and forceful expulsion of part or all of the stomach's contents. Vomiting rids the body of bolted food that may be hard to digest and spoiled (often scavenged) food that might make the cat ill.

Vomiting may be due to

- Overeating or eating too quickly
- Hairballs
- Poisoning from spoiled or bacteria-ridden food
- Poisoning from household or garden chemicals
- Worms or parasites
- Stomach ulcers
- Irritable Bowel Disorder
- Viral disorders
- Diabetes
- Cancer
- Kidney disorders
- Liver disorders
- Infectious diseases
- Hereditary conditions of the esophagus. The valve at the top of the stomach may be defective and this condition can worsen with age.
- Over-activity after a meal.
- And even stress or excitement.

Sometimes the cat will eat grass to promote vomiting. But grazing your lawn does not mean the cat will be sick. She may be seeking roughage or nutrients missing from the regular diet. Or perhaps, she just likes the taste. Make sure your cat has access to grass (free of chemicals). If she is an indoor cat, grow some wheat grass or oat grass in a flowerpot.

Vomiting is hard on the body and it is particularly stressful to the declining cat. The convulsions place a great strain on the cat's system, use valuable energy, and contribute to dehydration.

If your cat vomits, provide clean, fresh water so she can rehydrate.

Cats may become more sensitive to some of their food as they age—and throw it up. Try a different brand with substantially different ingredients; check the nutrition label. Avoid food coloring and preservatives.

Occasional vomiting in cats is normal. A repeated (four or more times a day) inability to keep food down is not. If the regurgitation lasts more than 24 hours *or* is accompanied by diarrhea, lethargy or refusal to eat, visit the vet. Blood in the vomit is a danger signal.

If the cat has an unsettled stomach or ate something that did not agree with her, your vet may prescribe smaller meals or a different cat food. On the other hand, your vet may find a more serious reason for the vomiting. Time is of the essence. The earlier the vet diagnoses the problem, the better the chance that treatment will be successful.

Hairballs (fur balls) cause most vomiting. Cats spend a lot of time grooming themselves. They swallow a lot of hair and expel a lot of hairballs out one end or the other. When the hair does not pass through, it accumulates and comes back up.

Look for lumps in the vomit. The cigar-shaped masses of compressed fur and saliva will appear gray regardless of the color of the cat. Some hairballs take on the color of recently ingested food—especially if the kibble is colored with red dyes. Regular brushing will minimize hair ingestion. Hairballs are common with all cats, long hair and short.

Occasionally, hairballs cause intestinal blockage. Look for diarrhea, inability to defecate, swollen abdomen, loss of appetite or retching.

Your vet will analyze stool and blood samples and x-rays may be taken. For some vomiting, your vet may recommend a low-fiber diet but for hairballs, a high-fiber diet. Capsules of psyllium may be administered daily—with sufficient water. Also ask your vet about pumpkin for hairballs and constipation. If hairballs are a constant problem, the vet may prescribe nutritional supplements. The vet may also prescribe low-fat dry cat food or a vet-approved laxative to help your cat remove the hairball. Only in extreme cases will surgery be required.

Your vet may recommend a non-digestible fat-type substance such as a teaspoon of mineral oil, or half a teaspoon of petroleum jelly to lubricate the cat's digestive track. It may be difficult to convince the cat to swallow these. Try a half-teaspoon of melted butter each day for a few days. Or try the oil drained from a can of sardines. You may also use a hairball paste every-other day (read the label). Pleasantly flavored, your cat will lick it off your finger. Cut back on the kitty treats and encourage the cat to exercise. Your vet may also recommend some catnip.

Diarrhea is a warning sign that all is not right inside. The body is rushing excess fluids to the gastrointestinal tract and is cutting back on water reabsorption in the large intestine to hurry-along something it does not want. Diarrhea can lead to dehydration, which can lead to severe organ damage. If diarrhea persists for two  days, is bloody or is accompanied by other symptoms such as vomiting, it is time to visit the vet.

Diarrhea can be caused by many of the same things that induce vomiting. Some additional causes are sudden changes in diet, worms, parasites and vet-prescribed drugs such as antibiotics and steroids.

Many cats cannot properly digest cow's milk. Some milk and milk products give them diarrhea. Try Goat's milk.

Some cats naturally produce a soft stool while others make harder droppings. Check the color of the stool. White may indicate liver and pancreatic disorders. Light-colored blood may reveal a rectal disorder. If the blood is dark, there may be a disorder in the small intestine. Blood is a serious sign; it is time to visit the vet.

Dusty

Dusty was about 12 years old when we adopted her; we have enjoyed her company for about four years. About a year and a half ago, Dusty began to suffer from irritable bowel. Her intestines felt "ropy", according to the vet. Gradually, she began to lose weight and move very slowly. She would defecate large puddles, often missing her litter box. My wife would cry when she looked at her because we felt we were losing her. We actually considered putting her down rather than see her suffer.

I told my friend, Sandy, about the situation and she told me about the raw chicken diet. My wife researched the diet and bought the equipment needed to grind up the chicken. Dusty ate this new diet with wild abandon, knocking down several large servings at one sitting.

We watched as an amazing transformation took place, not all at once, but gradually. Dusty came back to us from the brink. She's got a lot of her personality back as well as some weight.

Obviously, she is an older cat and has been through a great deal. But I truly believe that without this diet, we would have lost her. Instead, she stands before us several times a day, making strong eye contact and demanding a good meal. Her

eyes are bright. Her coat looks good. And she has rejoined our clan, which consists of two other felines who are much younger than Dusty. She lets them know that she is still The Empress, so step aside.
—Dick Kline.

Take your cat and a stool sample (and a urine sample, if possible) to the vet. Your vet may draw a blood sample and do a full workup on the blood, stool and urine.

If your cat is seriously dehydrated, your vet may administer fluids intravenously or subcutaneously (under the skin) near the scruff of the neck.

If your vet determines the cause was simple food intolerance, he or she may prescribe withholding food for a day or so to let the cat's stomach settle down. The vet may also prescribe a low-fiber, low-fat diet.

Try fasting your cat for 24 hours and then changing to a bland diet to include boiled chicken, strained beef or lamb (baby food), cottage cheese, bread, plain yogurt or another cat food. Try mixing boiled hamburger or chicken with white rice, potatoes or pasta. Or, buy lamb & rice cat food.

Each time you feed your cat food or water, use a fresh, clean glass or ceramic bowl to avoid growing harmful bacteria.

Constipation occurs when fecal matter stops instead of passing on through the large intestine. The cat will become lethargic and strain trying to go.

Often the cat will cry in pain if you pick him up with your hands under his belly.

Constipation is usually caused by hairballs but may be due to other intestinal disorders.

The vet may administer fluids, give the cat a warm, soapy-water enema, try biological remedies and even massage. Occasionally, surgery is required.

Try raw liver or the oil drained from a can of sardines.

A cat is the only domestic animal I know who toilet trains itself and does a damned impressive job of it.
—Joseph Epstein, author.

Internal parasites (worms and protozoans) inhabit cats of all ages. Parasites rob your cat of vital nutrients, leading to reduced appetite, loss of energy, anemia and even death.

The parasites may be tapeworms, round worms, hookworms, heartworms, stomach worms, eyeworms or whipworms. Other internal parasites are the protozoans: Coccidia, Toxoplasmosis, and Giardia. Outdoor cats are more likely to be infected with parasites.

Tapeworms cause little or no symptoms in older cats though your cat may scratch or drag her bottom along the floor. The tapeworm's egg sacks break off and exit the cat through the anus. Look for the rice-like pouches sticking to the hair around the anal area. Fleas are sources of tapeworms. Try to eliminate fleas.

Some intestinal worms may venture from the anus at night. Use a flashlight to check the sleeping cat.

Take a stool sample to your vet annually and anytime you suspect parasites. Also note that roundworms, hookworms, tapeworms, and whip-worms are all contagious to humans. Use disposable gloves when handling stool and litter boxes.

Over-the-counter remedies are rarely strong enough to rid a cat of parasites. See your vet. Your vet will advise you on cleaning your home and yard to prevent reinfection.

Chapter Five

Medical Disorders

This chapter outlines some of the disorders common in older cats. The symptoms will help you discover the disorder earlier. Your vet's possible treatments will be listed and some home remedies will be mentioned. For homeopathic medicines, see the references in the appendix and

http://www.goodpet.com/.

Clear any medications with your vet before giving them to your cat. Some drugs may interact with each other with undesirable and unhealthy results.

Kidney disorders. The function of the two kidneys is to filter the blood and remove metabolic waste products via urine. If the toxins are not removed, the cat will become sick and die. Kidney disease must be diagnosed quickly and treated aggressively.

Kidney disorders are more common in certain breeds of cats such as Persians and Bengals. Diseases of the kidneys are more common in older cats.

Chronic Renal Failure (CRF) is a progressive, fatal illness that results from kidney disease that has been persisting for months or years. It may be caused by age, genetics or a tumor. With treatment, your cat can live for months or years. While cats can survive with as little as 30 percent kidney function, by the time you discover the disorder, he or she may have suffered significant kidney damage. Once the urea levels reach a certain threshold, death is inevitable, uncomfortable and often protracted.

Cats with mild CRF may not exhibit symptoms. Look for loss of appetite, loss of weight, vomiting, increased thirst, increased urination or incontinence, diarrhea, seizures, lethargy or bad breath. As the disease progresses, the symptoms will become more noticeable.

Monitor your cat's water bowl. While older cats tend to drink more water, great increases may indicate kidney malfunction.

Your vet may prescribe fluid therapy (intravenous or subcutaneous hydration) to flush toxins or diet modification (restricting protein, phosphorus and sodium) to reduce toxin formation. The vet will also treat the stomach ulcers that often develop. Kidney dialysis, a newer treatment in cats, is another possibility. Some kidney transplants have also been successful in cats.

Sappho

Sappho died 2½ years ago; at 18 years old. She was a friend who saw me through many changes. Her kidneys were malfunctioning and during the last two years of her life we gave her about a cup of fluids daily under her skin (using an iv setup). I was buying the fluids by the case to get a reasonable price. Sappho fought the treatments at first, but I think she realized it was a life-or-death situation and she co-operated after a few weeks. When she had a stroke and became paralyzed, I nursed her for several days before taking her in for euthanasia. I realized when I was trying to feed her by an eyedropper and she could not eat what I gave her, that it was time to let her go.

—Cate Monroe, North Kingston, Rhode Island.
http://www.MoonMountainPub.com

Your vet may prescribe Fortekor. A daily tablet will normalize the blood pressure within the kidney and reduce urinary protein loss. Fortekor is not a cure but it will slow the progression of the disease. It may increase survival by as much as three times.

Ask your vet if you should reduce protein and phosphorous in the food while increasing calcium and vitamin A. Increase fluids. You want to unburden the kidneys as much as possible.

Feline Lower Urinary Tract Disorder (FLUTD) or Feline Urological Syndrome (FUS) can happen to cats at any age, although it is more prevalent in older cats and affects males more often than females. In the United States, most cases occur in the late winter and early spring. Some people think stress may be a cause but it is probably hormonal.

FLUTD includes

- Cystitis: bladder or urethra inflammation
- Urethritis: bladder or urethra infection
- Cancer or a tumor in the bladder or urethra
- Trauma to the urinary tract from an accident
- Stones: A build up of crystals or mineral deposits
- Urethral Plugs: A soft, malleable material containing minerals, blood, cells/cellular debris, and protein.

If your cat strains to urinate or tries frequently but is passing very little urine, check for a hard or full bladder and blood in the urine. The cat may howl in pain or even vomit. If she misses the litter box or licks her genital area, pay attention to urination. When a cat can't urinate, the kidneys can't function. The cat can die in 48 hours.

Many cats will hold their urine if their litter box is not kept clean.

Your vet will check for blockages, remove them if necessary and work on rehydration to flush out the bladder and reestablish electrolyte balances. If bacteria are present, the vet will use antibiotics. It may even be necessary to hospitalize the cat for catheterization and flushing.

The vet will probably prescribe a high-energy diet with restricted magnesium, calcium and phosphorous as well as ingredients to adjust the pH of the urine. Your vet will probably prescribe food with low ash content.

Encourage your cat to drink more water. Put out more water bowls around the house so the cat does not have to walk as far for a drink. Add water to the food. Drain canned tuna or clams and give the water to the cat. Try adding gravy to the water. Your cat may be switched to canned food, which has more water in it than dry food. You can even make slurry of the canned food by adding water. More exercise will often help.

Incontinence. Although commonly used to describe uncontrolled urination, "incontinence" is a generic term covering fecal incontinence and unitary incontinence. Where both occur, it is double incontinence.

Uncontrolled urination is common in older cats. Incontinence could be dribbling after urination or from time to time throughout the day. It is not the same as excessive urination, marking, or spraying.

A man has to work so hard so that something of his personality stays alive. A tomcat has it so easy, he has only to spray and his presence is there for years on rainy days.
—Albert Einstein (1879-1955).
German-American physicist and Nobel Prize winner.

Incontinence occurs when the sphincter muscles around the urethra weaken and allow some urine to pass. Incontinence can also occur as a result of stress, disease or infection to the urinary tract, stones, spinal cord injury, brain injury, stroke or other neurological problems.

Depending on the reason for the dribbling, your vet may operate or provide medication.

Feed your cat vet-approved cat food. Make sure she is in a stress-free environment especially around the litter box.

Cleaning up
Incontinence or feebleness means that your feline companion fails to make it to the litter box in time. A product we found very helpful for clean up is an enzyme-based product called Nature's Miracle (I think now there are other similar products out). Spraying it on the offended spot works to remove the odor. We used a huge quantity of the stuff when our aging Sam and later Macbeth were in their last months. This is the sort of stuff the professional rug cleaners use and it's quite effective.

I've found it's also good for removing many food stains.
—Pat Bell, Eden Prairie, Minnesota.
http://www.catspawpress.com

Sweet Pea for Cats is an enzyme that was developed to stop odors at their source instead of just covering them up. See http://www.nitron.com/html/home___pet.htm

Arthritis. A cat can jump as much as seven times its own height. If the cat's joints become painful, his or her mobility will be reduced. .

Your cat may become less active, may limp or may stand after a nap and "freeze." The cat will wonder what is happening and you may wonder if the cat thinks you are causing the pain for some reason. Your cat may even run a fever, lose his appetite or howl from pain during movement.

Cats are subject to two kinds of arthritis.

Osteoarthritis is the most common. It is a degenerative condition of the cartilage covering the ends of the bones. It occurs with age and usage of the joints but it can occur in younger cats following a significant disease or some type of trauma to the joints such as being attacked by another cat.

Rheumatoid arthritis is rarely seen in cats. It is an autoimmune condition in which the body attacks the cat's own joints and tissues and results in arthritis.

Your vet may x-ray the cat to look for arthritis and may draw a blood sample to check for cancer. The x-ray procedure often requires sedation to immobilize the cat. Some cats require a general anesthetic and a hospital stay.

The treatment your vet prescribes will depend on the type of arthritis your cat has and may include antibiotics, anti-inflammatory drugs or steroids. The vet may prescribe glucosamine/chondroitin supplements.

Apollo
Apollo had been relatively healthy, but had his share of illnesses. In his older years, he had become arthritic and had trouble jumping up and down. I made a number of small stools out of plywood and placed them strategically near favorite resting places, my bed, the sofa, etc. so the cat could step up as necessary. One particularly difficult need involved his litter box, which was kept in the "second" bathroom bathtub.

When it became difficult for him to jump, I placed stools of graduated heights in a row allowing an easy climb up to a plywood sheet at the foot of the tub, then another stool to step down to before stepping off into the litter box. He was quite happy with this arrangement. He lived 19 years.
—Pete Masterson, El Sobrante, California.
http://www.aeonix.com

To reduce swelling and promote healing, apply a compress soaked in a solution of water and apple cider vinegar (4:1) to the affected joint.

Buy common cod liver oil gel capsules, punch or cut a hole in one end and squirt the contents on some kitty treats. Or, hold the cat's head, press the capsule against the side teeth and squirt the contents into the mouth. Check with your vet. You do not want to give the cat a vitamin A overdose. Most cats like the fish product and the oil will lubricate the joints. Yes, it works for humans too. If home remedies are not making the cat comfortable after two days, visit the vet.

Liver disease. Cats can get five different types of liver disease that lead to liver damage. The liver is resilient and can even regenerate itself a bit but by the time you discover a problem, the liver may be 70-80 percent damaged. The symptoms of liver disease are not unique because liver problems are often part of other illnesses. Liver disease often occurs to cats that are overweight.

Fatty liver disease or hepatic lipidosis occurs when fatty deposits build up in the liver. When the cat stops eating for some reason, usually in conjunction with another disease, the body will start to use the fat stores for fuel. Unfortunately cats are not very good at using stored fat for energy and fat can begin to accumulate in the liver. Just a few days of not eating may damage the liver.

Look for appetite loss, vomiting, diarrhea, weight loss, lethargy, irritability, swollen belly, yellowing of the skin or seizures. Check for a light, clay-colored stool and a darkly discolored urine.

Your vet will check the blood and may perform a liver biopsy. He or she may suggest ways to stimulate the cat's appetite and food intake to allow the liver to start functioning normally again. Once the cat is getting calories from food, it will not be necessary for the body to break down fat for energy.

Your vet may prescribe an appetite stimulant such as Milk Thistle or Valium. Your cat may also be put on a course of drug therapy consisting of antibiotics, anabolic steroids and possibly immunosuppressive medications.

Your vet may suggest restricting protein, fat and sodium. Feed the cat cooked liver, fish, dairy products, cottage cheese or tofu. Mix them with cooked (but not wild) rice. If the cat is overweight, the vet may suggest a low-fat, high-fiber diet.

Caught early and treated properly most liver disorders are correctable and survivable.

Heart diseases may cause the heart muscle to enlarge, putting a strain on the heart. As the heart loses its ability to pump blood, other organs are affected.

Look for irregular or rapid breathing, weakness, lethargy, coughing or abdominal swelling. Get the cat to the vet.

Ask your vet about coenzyme Q-10 for heart conditions.

Annie

Annie was suddenly stricken and was exhibiting symptoms of fast panting along with paralysis of the rear legs.

As this was on a Sunday evening, we rushed her to the emergency 24-hr. vet in Berkeley, where the diagnosis was a heart attack followed by a blood clot on the spine. The emergency doctors weren't particularly helpful with a prognosis. I decided that prolonging the frightening procedures with a very uncertain result would simply extend the suffering, so I elected to end her suffering at that time. [This cat had joined my household after having been abandoned (as an adult) by it's previous owner. She showed behaviors that may have indicated previous trauma and was a "scaredy cat," becoming very upset with handling, etc.]

Later, in discussing the situation with our regular vet, it appeared that the "correct" decision had been made, as the

outcome of "aggressive" treatment in similar cases was usually ineffective at changing the eventual outcome.
—Pete Masterson, El Sobrante, California.
http://www.aeonix.com

Upper Respiratory Infection is a "kitty cold" or flu. Cats with colds often lose their appetite and a cat that does not eat for a few days can risk organ damage.

You will see reddened and runny eyes and a runny nose. Your cat will wheeze, sneeze, lick her nose and may have trouble breathing. Unfortunately, cats are not good at blowing their noses. While kitty colds are similar to human colds, cats and people cannot catch colds from each other. Colds are, however, contagious between cats just as they are between people. The incubation period is one to four days. Upper respiratory infections may take a few days to two weeks to clear up.

Persians and cats with flattened faces may suffer more severely from respiratory tract ailments.

Older cats tend to be more resilient and recover from colds sooner than kittens. Colds are not terribly serious but they can lead to secondary infections while the cat is in a weakened state. When your older cat has a cold, be aware of other disorders.

Your vet will check the cat's temperature and may prescribe antibiotics, decongestants, antivirals, supplements, rest, and lots of food and liquids.

It may also help to humidify the nasal passages. You can purchase a room humidifier or take the cat into a steamy bathroom.

Keep your cat warm. Maintain 70 degrees (F) in the room where the cat is. Also keep the cat dry; towel off the cat if she becomes wet. Talk to your vet about yearly vaccinations and supplements to ward off such infections. A cat with an untreated kitty cold may stop eating or may develop a case of pneumonia.

Allspice

When Allspice, a sealpoint Siamese, was 11½ or 12, it became obvious that he was laboring to breathe. This appeared to be the same as what had happened to his littermate Paprika some 5 years earlier when we found out that she had a cancerous tumor that was creating fluid in her chest cavity, leaving little room for her lungs. Had he had the same problem as his littermate, I had already made up my mind that I would not use the expensive cancer medication that had not done her any good.

As it turned out, his problem was something the vet said she had never seen—the air sacks in his lungs were bursting, leaving him less and less lung capacity. The first indication to us was that he labored when he went up stairs. He had to stop every few stairs to catch his breath. I usually picked him up and carried him up.

After a very expensive $600 stay at the vet's office, I took him home, saying that he would have to live or die under my ministrations. It was with Allspice that I learned about Pedialite and stale 7-Up. When I brought him home from the vet he was quite limp and he would not eat or drink water. In desperation, I prayed for an answer. It came to me to give him some 7-Up and Pedialite—something I had just heard about in an advertisement. I mixed the two roughly 1:1 and gave it to him with an eyedropper at the back of his mouth. If I remember correctly, I gave him four full droppers every hour. Within four to six hours, there was a marked difference.

Then I called a local health food store and asked what they would recommend for a person who was having trouble breathing. It was recommended that we use ground Mullein leaves for the breathing problems, ground Hawthorne berries in case the breathing problem was contributed to by a bad heart, along with powdered natural vitamin C with bioflavinoids for better metabolizing/absorption. I had him mix them in even parts by weight. I bought some large gelatin capsules. I filled the capsules by stabbing them open-end down into the ground mixture. I started out by giving him two capsules twice a day (at meal times). The difference was amazing. Within a couple of days he was running up the stairs again. Later I cut the dosage down to one capsule twice a day and then only when he exhibited problems breathing.

As a direct result, we were gifted with an extra 2 to 2½ years with him. And he had a good quality of life, except for being forced to take capsules. But, somehow he knew they were saving his life and didn't fight too hard until the last.

I believe, and the vet concurred, that he died of kidney failure. Was it brought on by large doses of herbs over the last years of his life? No one knows. But I do know that his life would have been shorter if I hadn't started giving him herbs. I told the breeder from whom I had gotten Allspice that he had died. It turned out that he had lived the longest of that particular litter—the last litter birthed by his kitty mom.
—Jacque Foreman, Altadena, California.
http://www.abacus-es.com/foreman

Ask your vet about making a saline solution with a few drops of golden seal root herb. It may be used to shrink and open blocked nasal passages.

Pneumonia is an infection of the lungs and is often the complication of some other disease.

Look for wheezing, sneezing, difficult breathing, coughing producing yellow-green sputum or blood, shortness of breath, lack of appetite, lack of energy and/or fever.

Your vet may take x-rays and check the blood. He or she may prescribe antibiotics and other medications depending on the underlying cause. Make sure the cat drinks enough water.

Allergies. As cats mature, they become more sensitive to their environment.

Fleabites cause skin problems and are the source of internal parasites such as tapeworms and round-worms. Flea collars, while convenient, are less effective than powders or sprays. Some cats are sensitive to the collars themselves.

Cats can also be allergic to molds, pollen, plants and household chemicals. Some 5 to 10 percent of cat allergies are due to food.

Look for scaly, scabby or inflamed skin, persistent scratching, loss of hair or skin infection.

Your vet will run allergy tests to determine the allergen. Then your cat can either undergo desensitization to the allergen or simply avoid it. Your vet will probably suggest replacing existing protein sources with hypoallergenic protein such as is found in lamb, rabbit, turkey and duck.

Diabetes is more likely in older cats (8 to 13 years) than younger animals. Overweight cats are at greater risk. There are two types of diabetes. Both Type I and Type II can lead to kidney damage, blindness, coma, and death.

✔ **Type I** (not enough insulin) diabetes is the most serious and it affects 50 to 70 percent of cats diagnosed with diabetes. About one in every 500 cats gets Diabetes Mellitus (DM) or "sugar diabetes." There is no cure for this disorder so insulin must be supplied through injection under the skin or in pills.

✔ **Type II** (too much insulin) diabetes is less serious than Type I. This type can be found in older cats that have been consuming too many sugars (carbohydrates) over a long period of time. Check the composition of kitty treats. A cat that has to lose weight may be put on a high-fiber, low calorie diet.

Look for excessive thirst or urination, diarrhea, dehydration, lack of energy or increased appetite with weight loss.

Ramses

Some years ago, Ramses, a male Siamese (named after the Egyptian Pharaoh), gained a lot of weight and tipped the scales at 26 lbs. We put him on a diet but the fewer calories he got, the less he moved. (Vet asked, "...has he been lethargic?" Answer: "I don't know; he never moves!")

Finally, his weight suddenly plummeted. (He is still fat, but "only" weighs 16 lbs. now.) After some tests, we found that the cat had become diabetic. He is now on insulin, receiving two shots per day for the past 10 years. Cats really like a routine. He has incorporated the shots into the schedule. (He gets a shot, then he gets a meal—not a bad deal.) I've trained him to jump up onto a dining room chair to make it easier to administer the shot. He only flinches or complains (with a sharp OW!) in the rare event that the needle hits a "sensitive" spot. It's important to vary the injection spot to avoid creating scar tissue or subcutaneous irritation that might interfere with the absorption of the insulin.

A side effect of the diabetes is a greater tendency toward bladder infections. (Unlike humans, taking the numerous daily blood checks to closely monitor insulin dosage is not practical in cats, so high glucose blood levels can lead to sugar in the urine... making it a more favorable place for bladder infections to flourish.) During these bouts, it is necessary to give him oral medication in the form of pills.

—Pete Masterson, El Sobrante, California.
http://www.aeonix.com

Your vet will test the blood or urine for glucose (sugar) levels to see if the pancreas is producing sufficient, but not too much, insulin.

A high-fiber diet may be prescribed to regulate the rate at which nutrients are taken into body cells. Several small meals each day will keep blood sugar levels more consistent.

Cancer. Cats, especially older cats, do get cancer. Cats develop cancer somewhat less often than dogs and humans. But cancer is the cause of death of nearly half the pets over 10 years of age.

Cancer cells are normal ones that suddenly go out of kilter. They tend to grow and spread throughout the body. There are many types of cancer in cats: skin, breast, head, neck, lymphoma, feline leukemia complex, testicular, abdominal and bone. Many times cancer can be treated successfully.

Search the cat's body for lumps and watch for loss of appetite, difficulty in eating/swallowing, weight loss, vomiting, changes in the fur, blood in the urine, urine or stool changes, diarrhea, incontinence, bad breath, difficulty breathing, discharges from any body opening, wounds that fail to heal or overall weakness.

Nick
Nick loved the sun. He'd sit for hours, basking in the warmth and complaining only when the mocking birds dive-bombed his peace. It was the sun that killed him. Nick had no pigment in his nose. Years of California sun did what it does to sunbathers of all species. We should have known—sores that

don't heal and all that. Eventually we took Nick to the vet, who said, "I could have this biopsied, but I can tell you what it is." Nick had cancer of the nose. Dr. Rose offered to operate.

We decided not to. Nick had suffered brain damage when the car hit him. He couldn't judge distances anymore. We chose instead to let him tell us when it was time to go.
—Robert Goodman, San Diego.
rg@SilverCat.com

Your vet will use blood tests, x-rays, biopsies and ultrasound to check for cancer. Treatments include drugs, surgery, chemotherapy, radiation, dietary supplements and immunotherapy.

Dental problems are manifested by chewing difficulties, loss of appetite, bleeding soft gums, bad teeth, loose teeth, bad breath, drooling, gum disease, dark spots on molars and raised sores in the mouth. If your cat has difficulty eating or grooming, it could be due to dental disorders.

Regular dental examinations are recommended as dental problems can go undetected for months. If left untreated over a long period of time, bacteria from a mouth disorder can get into the cat's bloodstream damaging the kidneys, heart and liver.

Dry cat food provides an abrasive for teeth and helps to keep them clean. Kitty treats such as Whiskas Dentabits are shaped and textured to clean a cat's teeth.

On the other hand, as cats grow older they may experience dental disorders that make it difficult for them to eat crunchy food. In this case, the dry food is swallowed whole only to cause indigestion and vomiting of the unchewed kibble. Most cats manage very well without teeth if given soft food.

Taking care of a cat's dental disorder, such as removing a bad tooth, will often give the cat a new lease on life. With the pain gone, the cat suddenly becomes interested in food and play again.

Thyroid disorders may be hyperthyroidism (overactive) or hypothyroidism (underactive).

Hyperthyroidism is when the thyroid produces too much thyroid hormone.

The thyroid may be enlarged as the result of a tumor or the gland itself may be enlarged. Hyperthyroidism is the most common hormonal disorder in older cats.

Hyperthyroidism speeds up the metabolism, changing the rate at which the body burns calories and may, in turn, damage the heart and kidneys. Left untreated, it can lead to heart, kidney or liver failure.

Chica
My cat Chica, a 13-year old tortoise-shell adopted from the ASPCA as a kitten, has been a loyal and loving pet, a little on the crabby side, but our own kitty nonetheless. She commutes with us to our weekend house in the country and puts up with a fair amount of harassment from members of the household. About two or three months ago, she stopped eating (she had always been a pig), and/or threw up her food (not due to the usual hairballs or eating grass thing). She was being finicky. She

was more lethargic than usual. Then, about a month ago, she ceased eliminating, first feces and then urine. I really got worried, and made an appointment for her at the vet. The other thing she started to do was drag her rear legs, almost like she was too tired to walk.

At the vet (where she has a really "bad rep"—chart says, "attack cat"), she was so unlike herself; she barely hissed at the vet. Her temperature was normal, and her x-ray showed no blockage (which is what I had suspected) and no major abnormality. They took blood. Chica and I went home and waited.

The vet called a few days later, and asked about Chica's health. He was sure I was going to report her demise. He told me that according to the blood test, her thyroid reading was 25.00, as opposed to .80, which is normal. She was EXTREMELY hyperthyroid. Treatment involved giving her pills (Tapazole, 5 mg twice a day) and believe it or not, after about three or four days, Chica perked up and ate with zest. The vet had told us to tempt her with honey-ham, fresh tuna, home-cooked chicken, and chicken liver. She was in heaven; it was practically a resurrection.

The problem remains...the pills. She hates them. We've utilized the "three people holding her down and jamming a pill down her gullet" method, but nobody is too happy about it. Then my son discovered a method of hiding a pill in a Bonkers treat, which worked for about a week until the pill popped out and Chica announced to us that "the jig was up." The vet says I could take her to the Animal Medical Center in Manhattan and irradiate her (and they would have to keep her until she was no longer radioactive) to the tune of $1K or more, or keep shoving pills. So for now, it's pill shoving. Sometimes she seems to understand, even though she doesn't like it. Sometimes she's just plain pissed off. We are delighted though

that she has bounced back, and now that spring is here, Chica is practically acting kittenish, checking out the birds, the blossoms and the trucks passing.
—Robin K. Blum, Brooklyn, New York.
http://www.InMyBook.com

Symptoms of hyperthyroidism are similar to that of some types of cancers, kidney disease and diabetes. Look for nervousness/hyperactivity, repeated vomiting, weight loss in spite of eating more, increased thirst, increased urination, rapid heartbeat, unkempt fur, increased appetite or diarrhea.

Your vet, with a simple blood test, can positively diagnose a thyroid disorder. A biopsy of the thyroid gland may also be performed. Treatment includes radioactive iodine treatment (effective but expensive), surgical removal, and oral medication (pills).

✔ **Hypothyroidism**, on the other hand, is when the thyroid is not producing enough thyroid hormone. It is very rare in cats.

The symptoms are hair loss, dry skin, weight gain, lethargy and irritability.

Your vet can correct the problem with hormone supplements.

The best precaution is early detection and treatment. For more information, see the Cat Thyroid Center at http://www.catthyroid.com/

Senility sneaks up on cats just as it does humans. The senile cat may be forgetful of his own well-being. He may venture into risky areas, be unable to find his way back home, not remember to come in from the rain or be unable to find the litter box.

Obviously, this cat should be confined to the house or an escape-proof yard.

Your vet will determine whether the behavior is due to a physical challenge or senility.

Feral (un-homed) cats rarely live long enough to become senile. When their minds do begin to slip, they become easy prey for predators.

Strokes rarely happen to cats and when they do happen, recovery is usually fast. The cat may have a lopsided appearance but will be near normal. Cats are very resilient.

Saddle Thrombus is a form of thromboembolism and is not uncommon in older cats. It is a blood clot that catches in the artery serving the hind legs at the point where the artery splits. Saddle Thrombus restricts or blocks the flow of oxygenated blood to the muscles in the hind limbs. Even if the cat recovers, a health threat still exists because fragments of the clot are in the circulatory system and may enter the lung, heart or brain.

The cat may walk on its hocks due to muscle damage. Some cats survive for several years under veterinary supervision.

Seizures are a sudden, uncontrollable and often violent thrashing of the body produced by an involuntary contraction of the muscles. The cat may fall down and lose bladder and bowel control. Be careful. A cat in seizure may scratch and bite; cover him with a towel and restrain.

A seizure is a sign that something is very wrong with your cat. Seizures are also dangerous in and of themselves as the cat can choke and hurt himself during the seizure.

Seizures occur for a variety of reasons: head injuries, disease, infection, tumor, kidney failure, allergy, epilepsy and poisoning. So it is important to learn the reason *behind* the seizure to decide on appropriate treatment.

See the vet for any seizure. If the seizures lasts more than two minutes or if they occur more than once in 24 hours, make an *emergency* visit to the vet.

There are many different types of seizures. You can help your vet to determine the type and be better able to find the cause by recording as much as possible about the seizure. When your cat has a seizure, take note of every detail.

Rabies is an acute viral infection of the central nervous system. Animals in the wild including raccoons, skunks, coyotes, and foxes usually carry it. If another animal bites your cat, young or old, check for rabies.

It takes four to eight weeks for your cat to show signs of being bitten by a rabid animal. At first, your cat will act strangely. He or she may become restless, excitable and may disappear for long periods. Then the cat will go into body spasms, become aggressive and even paralyzed.

Your cat should have a rabies vaccination between three and six months of age. After that a rabies booster can be given every three years. There is no cure for rabies and the usual course of action for a rabid cat is euthanasia.

Poisoning. Many things around your home are toxic to your cat. House plants such as cacti, human food such as chocolate, household cleaners and so on.

If your cat scratches at her face or mouth or rubs her mouth on surfaces, she may have ingested something poisonous. Look for behavioral changes such as increased salivation, dry mouth, lethargy, restlessness, vomiting or muscle tremors. Place your ear to the cat's side to monitor respiration and heart rates.

Poisoning is not necessarily fatal; it may only make the cat sick. The effect of the toxic material will depend upon the substance, the amount and what else was ingested as well as the size, age and health of the cat.

As with humans, inducing vomiting may do more harm than good. It is better to call the vet and get the cat to the emergency room as soon as possible.

Contact the Animal Poison Control Center toll-free at 888-426-4435. They are available 24/7. There is a $45 charge per case (have your credit card ready). See http://www.napcc.aspca.org/. You can also call 911.

The Animal Poison Control Center or your vet may recommend Milk of Magnesia: One teaspoon per five pounds of body weight mixed with water. Or, 25-50 grams (.88 to 1.76 ounces) of activated charcoal powder mixed with water. Feed one ml (.033 fluid ounces) per pound of body weight.

No one knows your cat's behavior as well as you. Keep a monitoring eye on your cat. Early detection is the most valuable treatment for most any disorder.

The Lifetime Costs of a Cat
©Dan Poynter

A cat is an investment; there are costs and rewards. Stephen Zawistowski, Ph.D., Senior vice-president of the ASPCA in New York has calculated the costs of raising a cat from birth through the average 16-year life. The cost will vary with the cat's size, health (no major medical bills), lifespan and choices between burial and cremation. The costs per year break down as follows:

$200-250   Food, dry kibble
$125   Vet visits
$200-250   Kitty litter
$200   Accessories: Bowls, brushes, carriers, litter boxes, etc.
$15-20   Toys and treats
$795   Total annual cost

Over 16 years, that works out to $12,720 or $2.18 per day. By the way, the costs of a second cat are lower. Many of the items may be shared except for food and vet bills.

Now just what do you get for your money?

☑ Naming rights. You may give her a single name or two or just call her "Kitty."

☑ Glimpses of God's work every day. Your angel here on earth.

☑ Endless purring and Velcro hugs.

☑ Photographs of playtime secured to the refrigerator with magnets.

☑ A front-row seat to history to witness her first mouse, the pride of successful potty training and her discovery of the cat in the mirror.

☑ Endless wonder over string, bugs and running water.

☑ An education in feline psychology, organs of the body, animal nutrition, waste management and communications.

☑ A furry friend to wake you up on cold nights with demands to get under the covers.

☑ She lets you know that she knows the difference between a can of freshly opened, warm cat food and yesterday's cold food from the refrigerator.

☑ Finding that cats age better than people because their fur hides the wrinkles.

☑ Finding and saving her baby teeth and not being subjected to Tooth Fairy extortion.

☑ Teaching her to jump on the bed rather than clawing her way up, by trimming her nails.

☑ Being envious of the luxury of being able to stare out a window for hours.

☑ Laughing when she first discovers her tail.

☑ Doing the math to discover that your 12-year old cat is 55 in people years but that since she naps 18 hours each day, she slept through 75 percent of her years of both kinds.

☑ Being a hero for retrieving a toy from the roof, getting her down from a tree, chasing off the neighborhood dog, bringing home a new bag of kitty litter, blotting car grease out of her tail, and giving her kitty treats just for the asking.

☑ Having enough shredded fur to make a wardrobe of sweaters.

🐈 Admiring her ability to find the warm spot in any room—often on top of the TV with the tail hanging down in front of the screen.

🐈 Accepting her kneading you and sometimes drooling to demonstrate acceptance as her caretaker.

In the eyes of your cat, you are both mother and dad—you rank right up there with God. You have the authority to provide food, the power to heal and the right to share unconditional love. Your cat will love you absolutely, even when you are upset, without counting the cost.

Chapter Six

Nutrition

In an average year, cat guardians in the United States spend more than $2 billion on prepared cat food. We do not have figures on the number of cats that regularly "eat out" on birds, rabbits, lizards and mice.

As a cat matures, nutrition becomes more important. The digestive system grows to be less efficient; these changes begin to take place at around seven years. Sometimes a simple change of diet will improve your cat's health.

Older cats are prone to disorders of the liver, constipation, and inflammatory bowel disease. These older cats need food containing easily digested protein.

Your aging cat should have several smaller meals each day instead of two main meals.

There is disagreement on whether a cat should eat raw meat or prepared cat food. Many cat nutritionists prefer balanced-diet dry foods as long as the cat has healthy teeth. They argue that mice bear fleas and uncooked meat contains harmful bacteria.

 On the other hand, some professionals recommend a natural diet citing Dr. Francis Pottenger's study of cats between 1932 and 1942. One group of cats were fed raw food and the other groups were fed various combinations included heated or cooked foods. The first generation of these cats, eating prepared foods, developed degenerative health disorders (arthritis, allergies, diabetes, etc.) near the end of their lives. The disorders occurred earlier and to a greater degree in the second- and third-generation cats. See

http://www.price-pottenger.org/   &   http://www.blakkatz.com/potscats.html

But, not everyone agrees

http://www.beyondveg.com/tu-j-l/raw-cooked/raw-cooked-1h.shtml#pottengers

I believe feeding a diet of fresh food—namely raw meat and supplements helps keep cats young and vital. Commercial food is loaded with preservatives, coloring and who knows what else. Over the years, this builds up in a cat's body. Think of what condition you would be in if you ate nothing but cooked food and processed food.
—Michelle T. Bernard, Boston, Massachusetts.
http://www.blakkatz.com

The cats on the all-raw diet maintained optimum health with each generation. They had good bone structure, excellent bone density, shiny coats, well-developed and spaced teeth, wide mouth structures, and did not have parasites or disease.

A mouse a day keeps the veterinarian away.

Many cat guardians find dry kibble to be more convenient than opening cans of wet cat food. A cat on dry food will drink a lot more water.

Canned food may be easier for the older cat to bite and swallow. Kibble can be made softer with gravy. A good variety of food may be better for the cat.

Even with dry food, you should use clean glass or ceramic bowls at each feeding to avoid bacteria buildup. Some people buy paper "boats" from restaurant suppliers to assure the food dish is always clean.

"Senior formula" cat foods provide easier-to-digest protein and fewer calories per portion for the less-active cat. Cooked chicken or fish as well as commercial "kitty candy" may be used for treats.

As a cat matures, her sense of smell deteriorates; your cat may become even more finicky. Try a stronger smelling food or warm it in the microwave oven to increase its aroma.

Cats love meat-based baby food such as Beechnut. Check the label and avoid baby food with onion powder.

**If your kitty will not eat baby food meat without coaxing, that
kitty is either very sick or has a bad case of hairballs.
—Jacque Foreman, Altadena, California.**
http://www.abacus-es.com/foreman

In the U.S., lamb-based cat foods are often promoted
at hypoallergenic. Until recently, sheep protein was
uncommon in North American cat foods. Sheep has
been a common cat food in the UK and is just as
likely to be an allergen as any other ingredient.

Dog food is formulated for canines. Raiding the dog
dish is OK occasionally, but a steady diet of dog food
can lead to the illness, blindness, and death of your
cat due to inadequate amounts of taurine, an amino
acid essential to cats.

Cats are carnivores; their
teeth are made for slashing,
not for grinding. They need
a meat-based diet. Seventy-
five percent of their daily
diet should be meat. Do not
limit your cat to vegetables
and grains.

Chapter Seven

Medical Care

The older cat should visit the vet every six months for a physical examination including diagnostic tests. For the mature cat, six months is equal to two years for a human. Weigh your pet and record the reading on each visit.

Just as with humans, the earlier you detect and treat an illness, the better the chances for recovery and life extension. Keep a critical eye on your older cat.

Keep a file or diary on your cat. Maintain all records such as the cat's shots, food, weight, respiration and temperature. If the cat becomes sick, injured or starts acting differently, record your observations in detail. Often cats act one way at home and another way in the vet's office. Your vet will need the information to determine the reason *behind* the disorder.

According to Purina's *State of the American Pet Survey*, 98 percent of cat guardians describe their cat's health as good. Some 84 percent say it is very good and 46 percent say they have not experienced any health problems with their cat.

Cat guardians report their cat's greatest health problems to be: hairballs (6 percent), fleas and ticks (5 percent), and urinary tract infections (4 percent). Three percent or fewer cat guardians mentioned each of any other health problems.

About 34 percent give their cat medicine while 26 percent take their cat to the vet. 62 percent of cat guardians say their pet's health problem has been solved. Some 27 percent of cat guardians say some progress has been made, but they are still working on a solution. But 11 percent of cat guardians say problems still exist.

For detailed advice on most cat diseases, see
http://www.21cats.org/health.html#0

Insurance. Most serious injuries and diseases can be treated but surgical operations and medication are usually expensive. To ease the possible economic burden, some people purchase pet insurance (see the appendix).

Natural remedies. Some pet guardians have considered or sought alternative health remedies. Some 26 percent of cat guardians have either considered or sought nutritional supplements for their pets. While 16 percent of guardians have considered or sought a massage. The number of guardians who have considered or sought nutritional supplements or massages for their pet is significantly higher for guardians whose pet is age 13 or older. Some sources of natural remedies for cat ailments are below. And see the appendix.

http://www.petmedicinechest.com/feline/default.asp
http://www.herbsnpets.com/
http://www.hillsideherbal.com.au/
http://www.morrills.com/

For information on massage, see
http://www.lovingtouchpetcare.com/ and
http://findhornpress.com/49.html

For information on Bach Flower Remedies for Animals, see http://findhornpress.com/48.html

Physical examination may include checking the stool, urine, blood and utilize biopsies, x-rays or scans.

Physiologic values for cats

◩ Normal body temperature is 101.4 degrees Fahrenheit but may range between 100 and 102.5. Use lubricating jelly and insert the (electronic plastic) rectal thermometer into the anus ¾ to 1 inch.

◩ Normal heart rate at rest is 160-240 beats per minute with an average of 195. Feel for the pulse on the inside of the thigh or place your ear on the cat's side.

◩ Normal respiration rate at rest is 25-30 per minute. Respiration will increase to 65-90 per minute when excited or immediately after exertion. Watch the chest or belly or place your ear to the cat's side.

These are just ranges. Measure, record and compare your readings over time.

The smallest feline is a masterpiece.
—Leonardo da Vinci (1452-1519)
Italian painter, sculptor, architect, and engineer.

Treating your cat at home may be less traumatic for the cat and less expensive for you. In cases of diabetes where daily injections are required, it may not be practical to make repeated visits to the vet. There are many things to consider before becoming a nurse to your cat.

☑ Ask your vet about side effects; they may outweigh the benefits of treatment.

☑ How much time will this course of treatment take and what is the schedule?

☑ Can I find someone to continue treatment when I have to travel?

☑ How often must your cat visit the vet? Does the vet make house calls?

☑ Can I afford this treatment? Did I purchase insurance?

☑ Will your cat cooperate with pills or injections? Will your cat resent you for *torturing* him or her?

Nick
Nick lost a fight with a car. We were gone, visiting friends halfway to Ensenada. He couldn't get into our apartment, so he went to our neighbor's home. They took him to the 24-hour vet clinic, where the doctor suggested that we put him away. In spite of his broken jaw, damaged teeth, and severe concussion, we couldn't.

The vet performed several root canals on Nick and reset his jaw. Nick ultimately became famous in veterinary circles as one of the first successes in the history of cat dentistry.

Years later, a colleague told me his wife had attended a veterinarian's convention and watched as the doctor talked about and showed slides of the work he had done on Nick.
—Robert Goodman, San Diego.
rg@SilverCat.com

To convert medication dosage measurements, see the online converter at
http://www.megaconverter.com/mega2/

Cats don't like change without their consent.
—Roger A. Caras, animal book author.

Dehydration. Cats need water, lots of water. Some 60-70 percent of a cat's body weight is made up of water. Water is essential for transporting essential nutrients throughout the body.

Your cat will lose almost as much fluid in the saliva during grooming, as it will in urination. Vomiting and diarrhea expel a great deal of water, making rehydration essential. Cats can also become dehydrated due to fever, infection, diabetes, and kidney disorders.

Look for frequent drinking, dry nose, mouth or eyes and lethargy. Conduct a pinch test. Lift the skin off the cat's back and pinch it. It should be elastic and bounce back. If skin recovery takes more than a second, the cat is probably dehydrated.

Cady
Cady was a sweet, affectionate, gray and white, short-haired cat with a cute pink nose. For 18 years, she was my constant

companion through many changes in my life: the move from New York City to Los Angeles, various job and relationship transitions, etc. So at 17, when Cady started to lose weight, to exhibit less energy, and to lap up water from her bowl too often, I took her to the vet to see what the problem might be.

The vet said it was all the result of a kidney disorder. She gave my cat a hydration treatment, and suggested that I start administering them at home—one bag every other day. Gazing at dear Cady, I wondered if I'd be able to do this. I remembered earlier challenges of trying to give her medications, and her triumphant moments over my will, such as when she had victoriously emerged out of a cardboard carrying case during a drive to the vet in the early years.

One of my suggestions for any cat guardian—but particularly for someone with an aging kitty—is to create a support network of other cat lovers. After going home with Cady that day, I called another writer, Laura, to see what she knew about hydration. Laura reassured me that Cady would learn to cooperate, and told me how she was able to make one of her many cats more comfortable during his last months with hydration. Laura also warned me to be aware of when I might be trying too hard to keep the cat alive (for selfish reasons)—to stay alert to Cady's quality of life, and to let my feline friend go when the right time came.

Cathy—a long-time neighbor two doors away—is another cat fan. She had fed Cady during my absences, and they were pals. Cathy agreed to come over for the first few treatments to help me learn to work with Cady. As we worked together, I noted how she reassured the cat during the hydration process with a gentle tone and kind words. After two initial treatments, Cathy stood to the side the next time as I worked with the cat alone. From then on, I was on my own. Initially I wrapped Cady in a towel to keep her still during the treatments, but eventually this wasn't necessary.

It is so touching to see how these wonderful little creatures know you are helping them. Occasionally Cady would be too impatient to work with (I'd try again later in the day), but most of the time she would stand still with a little encouragement. Once she was settled, Cady often would look up at me appreciatively as I held my arms around her while the fluid entered her body. She and I were very close during those treatments, and it felt good to be able to assist her in this way. The vet told me that I probably added an extra year to Cady's life. My effort was small in return for all that dear sweet Cady gave to me.

—Robin Quinn
robinquinn@aol.com

Your vet will determine the cause of the dehydration. If the cat is ill, the vet will treat the illness. If your cat is seriously dehydrated, your vet may administer fluids intravenously or subcutaneously (under the skin) near the scruff of the neck.

Cassidy
The beginning of a cat's life is a joyous time: all that curiosity and energy. With impossibly tiny whiskers and claws, these little bundles of fur race around at breakneck speed, only to stop and fall asleep almost instantly, curled up in your lap, purring contentedly. It's a wonder to behold.

What happens, though, when that tiny bundle of joy becomes an aging kitty with a myriad of health problems? I had the opportunity to share in such an experience with my beloved feline friend, Cassidy.

Cassidy did not come to me as a kitten. When I found this stray cat with the gorgeous, big blue eyes, he was already about 10 years old. Veterinarians can determine the approximate age of a cat by looking into their eyes and by looking at the condition of their teeth.

While Cassidy was no longer a youngster, he still had energy, and strength, and a zest for life. He quickly captured my heart and became my best friend.

By the time he was about 15 years old, his steady decline became increasingly apparent. Where once he could jump effortlessly onto the bed, now was a concentrated effort. Where once he would meet me at the door each evening to let me know it was dinnertime, now he would barely nibble at his favorite foods.

Toward the end of that year, Cassidy's kidneys started failing. His veterinarian suggested I start giving him fluid injections to combat the ensuing dehydration that often comes with kidney problems. A veterinary technician came to my home and taught me how to insert the needle. It was easier than I had imagined. People who knew me were amazed at my newfound skill, as I could never be considered a "nurse" type. The vet technician explained that the nape of a cat's neck has fewer nerve endings than in other areas of the body, so they really don't feel any pain. She was right. Cassidy gave no indication that the needle insertions bothered him in the least. I just bunched up the scruff of his neck with one hand and inserted the needle with the other. It was a little like sticking the needle into an orange: a bit of resistance and then it was in.

The milky colored bags of fluids contain a balanced electrolyte solution, often filled with potassium and sodium or a simple saline solution, depending on the cat's needs. Many cats, I was told, can get a weekly or twice-weekly injection and do well for years. In Cassidy's case, he needed daily injections almost immediately to keep him hydrated. Each bag of fluid was $6.50 and each needle was 50 cents.

Now, you would think that a cat would want nothing to do with these injections. Who could blame him? With Cassidy, it was a different story. He was a mellow kitty to begin with, but he became even more content during his daily rehydrating sessions.

It took five to six minutes to drain 200 cc; 20 percent of the bag. Every day, during those few minutes, Cassidy and I enjoyed some really peaceful, quality time together. He would sit, quietly purring, as I stroked him, telling him how much I loved him and how grateful I was that he had come into my life.

All too soon, it was time to say goodbye. At age 16, Cassidy passed away peacefully in my arms. As his beautiful blue eyes closed for the last time, I silently gave thanks for the time I was able to spend with him as he prepared to go on his journey to another place; a place without pain or sickness; a place of only peace and joy.

Everyone loves a cute, playful kitten. It's the mature cat, though, who can teach us so much about love and life and loss. We can all learn from their wisdom and dignity in the face of declining health.

I wouldn't have missed the time I was able to spend with Cassidy during the last few months of his life for anything. Something tells me he felt exactly the same way.
—Karen Stevens, Santa Barbara
http://www.AllForAnimals.com

Provide clean, fresh water. Cats have a specialized sense of taste. They are very sensitive to slight variations in the taste of water. Let tap water stand to vent off the chlorine or provide purified or distilled water. Some cats dislike the taste of plastic; use a glass or porcelain bowl.

Ramses and Fluids
Over the years, a couple of illnesses have resulted in Ramses becoming dehydrated. Because of my skill with the insulin syringes, the vet (after a brief lesson) has trusted me to administer lactated ringers solution subcutaneously. (This is a big convenience, since I would otherwise have to take the cat into the vet's office twice a day for this service.) The needles are considerably larger than the insulin syringes, but the principle is the same. I can usually just hold the cat in my lap for the 15 or 20 minutes necessary to input the 100-150 cc of the typical requirement. The cat usually is relatively calm with this procedure, especially if I gently brush him at the same time (he's a real sucker for a hair brush).
—Pete Masterson, El Sobrante, California.
http://www.aeonix.com

Once your cat is in decline, it may not have the strength to stand and lap up water. You can administer a few drops at a time into the side of the mouth with an eyedropper, syringe or turkey baster. Do not squirt in too much; you do not want to gag the cat.

Murphy was only three
Murphy was just 3 years old and five pounds when she was diagnosed with renal failure. My vet sent me home with a bag of fluids and needles and said "Make her happy." My directions were to give her 100 cc of fluids once a day. I was so freaked out that I moved in with my Mom (I pass out a the

sight of a needle). We did it slowly at first because we were scared that we would hurt her. We let her decide how to sit/lay. I did her fluids after the first year—all by feel, not by sight.

She responded well and wanted to go for a walk outside after each session (she was an indoor kitty). We would walk some nights for 1½ hours. My thought was to keep her happy.

We progressed and eventually got her weight up to 10 pounds, but she settled in around 9 pounds. She maintained that weight for four more years.

In the fourth year, we had to increase her fluid intake to 150 cc and we continued that until the end of her little life. The first day she wanted to bolt at 100, but I explained to her that she had to wait to 150 from now on. And she did. From that moment on, the level was 150 but not 151!
—Donna Babylon
Maryland

Hand feeding. Sometimes a cat that is ignoring food, will respond to the attention of hand feeding. Try small slivers of chicken or liver.

Dickens

A week ago my white cat Dickens needed surgery and when he came home he looked so pitiful. Nobody told me he'd be unable to move his hindquarters (from the anesthesia) for 4 days and wouldn't even be able to use his box on his own. I doubled a rectangular silk scarf and slipped it under his lower abdomen, to gently hoist his hips slightly when he needed to pee.

His dependence on me reminded me that when he was a tiny kitten he was extremely sick... didn't eat for 4 days, was curled up in such obvious pain and was leaving bloody stool in his box. These are three very bad signs. I was terribly upset when two veterinarians told me there was no hope for him, that I should just expect him to die; that and I should bring him in to be "put down". Instead, I started feeding Dickens very tiny bits of plain cooked chicken. He ate it... it stayed down. He wanted more.

Slowly he got better and I started giving him Waltham's canned chicken and rice. He thrived.

Almost six years later he is a healthy 18 lb. cat (on a diet). Very feisty and very protective of me, he sleeps on my bed in the crook of my knees and can growl and bark like a dog if he detects an intruder.

—Andrea Reynolds, Lake City, Pennsylvania.
http://www.AndreaReynolds.com

Giving Medications. Sooner or later, you will have to give your cat medication in the form of a pill, liquid, powder, or a shot.

☑ **Pills**. Force and deception are your only alternatives when administering pills; reasoning and explaining will not convince your cat to cooperate.

Ramses and Pills

To a cat, pills are considered a fate worse than death. When Ramses sees a pill, he immediately begins to drool copious quantities of saliva, and fights all efforts to pry his mouth open. His tongue immediately starts 'working' to push the unwanted pill back out of his mouth.

After many such struggles, I discovered that capsules went down much easier. The pills would tend to become very sticky when coated with the saliva, but capsules become slippery. So, if the medicine isn't available as a capsule, I just put the pills in empty gelatin capsules from the drug store. It's still a bit of a battle, but by acting quickly and with minimal warning, I can usually get a capsule on to the back of his tongue before the saliva flood begins.

—Pete Masterson, El Sobrante, California.
http://www.Aeonix.com

Place the palm of one hand under the cat's jaw or on the back of the head, whichever is easier. Place your thumb and middle finger in the sides of the cat's mouth. Gently tilt the cat's head back and hold the mouth open.

Take the pill between your thumb and forefinger of the other hand. Quickly place the pill as far back in the throat as you can. For some pills, it helps to quickly dip them in water for lubrication.

Shut the cat's mouth and keep holding the cat's head back slightly with one hand. Use the other hand to lightly massage the cat's throat for as much as 10 seconds to stimulate swallowing. Watch the cat to make sure she swallows before you release the head.

Blowing on a cat's nose will often make her swallow.

Crickie likes it
To control fleas, I decided to give Cricket yeast & garlic pills. It wasn't easy; the pills were quite large and rough textured. After several attempts, only a few of which were successful, I discovered he liked the taste of yeast and garlic. Then we

turned pill time into a game. I would roll them across the floor. Cricket would chase, pounce and eat them with enthusiasm.
—Dan Poynter
http://OlderCat.com

Keep an eye on the cat for a few minutes to make sure the pill is not returned to daylight. If your cat tends to vomit following pill administration, try feeding a kitty treat to put a good taste in her mouth.

A spoonful of yogurt makes the medicine go down.
Giving a cat a pill can be a dangerous experience; cats have claws and are usually pretty strong. They don't like having pills poked down their throats. But many, if not all, like cottage cheese or yogurt. A dollop of yogurt with the pill on top is usually slurped right down. (Powdered medicine should be as easily given.)

Yogurt is a particularly good choice if the cat is on a regimen of antibiotics; the bacteria in yogurt are helpful in replanting the flora in the gut that are wiped out by the antibiotic.
—Pat Bell, Eden Prairie, Minnesota.
http://www.catspawpress.com/

If you have trouble getting the pills back far enough, consider buying a "piller" or pill rod from your pet store.

Pilling Jasper
To get rid of any lingering parasites, Jasper was required to take a large, blue, oblong pill once a week for 20 weeks. With his certain history of abuse, I knew pilling him was going to be an ordeal so I was ready with several strategies. I couldn't swallow a pill 3/4 inch in length so I knew to cut it into quarters for him. I tried all the tricks: wrapping it inside a tiny piece of

shaved chicken, coating the pieces thickly with softened butter (cats love butter), soaking the pill pieces with drops of water to soften them. Jasper continued to fight me with his sharp claws and teeth.

Finally, I pulverized one of the pill quarters and mixed it well with a half ounce of tinned chicken-flavored cat food. The food had a light blue tint but he ate it eagerly. Four of these servings over the course of the day, each Sunday, got the entire pill into his system with no more fighting.
—Andrea Reynolds, Lake City, Pennsylvania.
http://www.AndreaReynolds.com

Try crushing up the pill and mixing it with the cat's food. Sticky baby food may be used to conceal pills. Cover the medicine. Cats often eat around the pill or ignore the food altogether.

Gem
Gem is a wild cat that gets pills three times a day and hated it. We give her pills with a piller and squirt a bit of baby food in her mouth to help her swallow. She does not run up and ask for her pills, but after three years she no longer argues. She loves the baby food treats.
—Leo Grillo, Acton, California.
D.E.L.T.A. Rescue

◀ **Liquids and liquefied food** may be administered with a syringe, turkey baster or eyedropper in the same manner as a pill. Hold the mouth open and squirt in a small amount at a time. If the cat dislikes the taste, you will have to hold the mouth closed and massage the throat to promote swallowing.

If the medicine is very liquid, you can try squirting small amounts between the teeth on one side of the mouth while holding the mouth closed. Do not squirt so much as to gag the cat.

Granny

I found granny very emaciated, dehydrated and probably within days of death at a fellow volunteer's house. She was suffering from an upper respiratory infection.

I took her home with me because she broke my heart. I knew that because she was old and a rescue; that no one would spend the money for proper veterinary care. No one seems to know her true age; estimates were 13-14 or 17+. I decided to try and save her and then to try and rejuvenate her by switching her to a raw Feline Future diet.
(http://www.felinefuture.com/).

After about five days of subcutaneous fluids, antibiotics and syringe feeding, she began to eat on her own. She was so weak, she could barely stand, was very wobbly and when she did have a BM, it was diarrhea.

As soon as she was eating a little on her own, I offered her Feline Future chicken recipe. She tried it but still did not eat enough to suit me so I continued to mix it with Beechnut baby food. After a week of mixing with baby food or tuna juice, I cut her back to Feline Future exclusively.

Granny is now eating Feline Future three times a day and her stools are perfect. She is more active, wants to get out of the sick room and is begging for attention. In just four weeks, she has become an affectionate cat, purring constantly and giving little love bites when I pet her.
—Sandy Aldrich.

✔ Powders. First try sprinkling the powder on a sheet of paper to see if the cat will lick it up. If not, try sprinkling it on, or mixing it with moist cat food. You may have to resort to folding some paper into a V to slide the powder in the mouth like a pill.

He who lives by medical prescriptions lives miserably.
—Proverb

✔ Shots will be administered into a muscle or under the skin (subcutaneously). Many people find it is easier to give a shot to a cat than a human because the fur hides the entry of the needle. Ask your vet to teach you the technique.

Photocopy this chart, fill in and take it to your vet

Symptoms/Observations

❏ Forgets her housetraining
❏ Vomiting
❏ Diarrhea
❏ Increased thirst
❏ Increased urination
❏ Changes in activity level (hyper or lethargic).
❏ Excessive panting
❏ Confusion or disorder
❏ Less interaction with family, withdrawn, decreased responsiveness.
❏ Decreased hearing
❏ Decreased vision
❏ Changes in skin and hair coat
❏ Changes in sleeping pattern
❏ Yowling
❏ Changes in appetite
❏ Weight changes
❏ Difficulty climbing or jumping, limping, stiffness.
❏ Stool: soft, liquid, foamy, gel-like or bloody.
❏ Other

Chapter Eight

The Last Days

Given a choice, we would like our cats to enjoy a long happy, disease-free life and then to die quickly and peacefully in their sleep. Of course, it would be nice to have some warning so that we could say goodbye.

Some old and sick cats crawl off into a closet or other dark place only to be found dead a day or two later. They often ultimately succumb to starvation and dehydration.

If the cat just disappears, you won't know if she wandered off and may show up again someday. Maybe she was inspecting a car with an open window and was carried off and discarded once discovered or maybe a coyote ate her.

Making your cat comfortable. Perhaps your cat is not in pain and you have decided to let him or her live out a natural life. Or, maybe you are postponing the decision to put the cat to sleep. In either case, you want to make your cat as happy and comfortable as possible.

The point may come when the cat is suffering a terminal disease such as cancer, kidney disorder or liver disease. The treatments will extend life, but there is no hope for a cure and the cat is in pain— truly miserable. Now you have to decide between quality of life and quantity of life. You may elect hospice-type care by discontinuing the aggressive treatments.

Many people feel that death is a natural cycle in life. It is better to let the pet die naturally in familiar surroundings. Since the disease can't be cured, they focus on making sure the disease does not cause the pet discomfort.
See http://www.HealthyPet.com/Library/bond-17.html

Palliative care is the active total care of patients whose disease is not responsive to curative treatment and eases the transition from life to death. It includes management of pain and physical symptoms, but goes beyond the physical to include the emotional suffering of the family.

Palliative care affirms life and regards dying as a normal process; it neither hastens nor postpones death. The goal of palliative care is to achieve the best quality of life for patients and their families.
See http://painlaw.org/palliativecare.html

Bedding. If you use a box, make sure it is large enough. Older cats do not curl up as tightly as they once did. Cats like warmth and if the cat is getting frail, he or she may not be generating much heat. Your pet store has heating  pads designed especially for pets. Or, try filling a jar or hot-water bottle with hot water and wrap cloth around it. See if the cat snuggles up to it for warmth.

Most cats enjoy lying in the sun where they get both warmth and vitamin D. During the winter, make a "Kitty Beach": shine full-spectrum heat lamps on a sheepskin.

Provide access to a sunny spot but always supply escape. Once your cat heats up, he or she will want to move to a shaded spot. Older cats are less resistant to heatstroke and dehydration.

Ramps. As your cat winds down, jumping up may be strenuous and jumping down may be dangerous. Provide a ramp or step. For example, place a box or suitcase next to your bed.

Food, water and the litter box should be placed closer to the cat's bed once she shows signs of decreased energy and mobility. Your cat needs water and has been trained to go potty only in designated areas. The cat will become frustrated and will expend valuable energy if she must walk great distances for water and elimination. If the food and litter box are too close, your cat may avoid one or both.

Claws. Older cats may not wear down or sharpen their claws as much as when more active. Overgrown claws may not retract completely and may snag on threads in bedspreads and other stitched materials. The cat will be troubled when snagging a claw and could even pull away and become injured. Overgrown claws may even interfere with walking. A mild trimming should solve this mobility challenge.

Exercise. Your cat will slow down as he matures but he still needs exercise to keep healthy. Until he grows weak, take your cat on walks around the house or yard. Encourage play with catnip toys.

Chapter Nine

Choices, Before & After Death

Euthanasia literally means "gentle death." Some people describe euthanasia as "putting kitty to sleep," "putting the cat down," "putting the cat out of its misery," "humane destruction," "destroying the cat," or even "murder."

Euthanasia is becoming common even with people. Of the 130,000 people who died in the Netherlands as long ago as 1990, 11,800 were helped to die by their doctors, according to *The Wall Street Journal*. Derek Humphry has written several books on the subject. See http://www.finalexit.org/dhumphry/

Euthanasia: gentle death, painful decision.
—Sarah Hartwell
English cat writer

Taking your cat's life will be the most difficult decision you will make during his or her lifetime. Even after weighing the benefits, you may have feelings of both guilt and responsibility.

Quality v. quantity and pain v. suffering. What if your cat is in constant pain, the stressful treatments are not really helping, she is uninterested in life and is not responding to affection? It may be kinder to put the cat to sleep than to make her endure further suffering.

Your vet will evaluate your cat's physical condition but only you can judge the way she acts—her quality of life. Pain can be medicated but suffering can get to the point where your cat wants you to stop all life support and let her go. If the cat is in an irreversible decline and in pain, you have the ability and even the responsibility to be merciful.

The paperwork. Your vet may ask you to sign a consent form giving permission to euthanize your cat. This is a legal document and should be taken seriously.

The procedure. Euthanasia is accomplished by injecting an anesthetic overdose. Your vet may relax the cat by feeding a pill or injecting a tranquilizer first. Once the shot is given, the cat will become unconscious almost immediately; death comes quickly and painlessly.

If you are cradling the cat in your lap or are just holding on, you will feel the cat exhale, relax and seem to become heavier. Urine may trickle from the bladder as the muscles relax.

In contrast, convulsions, hemorrhaging, pain, starvation and dehydration may accompany a natural death.

Thevenin's Decline

For the last couple of years our 16-year-old cat, Thevenin, had gotten the sniffles every winter, but we expected her to live several more years. After all, her day consisted of waking up, eating, getting petted, going back to sleep, and, when it wasn't too cold or wet, stepping outside to do her business.

This winter when the sniffles cropped up, the medicine her vet gave her didn't work. While concerned, we blamed it on her age. She had also developed difficulty going up and down stairs, and her hearing seemed to be affected as well.

Suddenly Thevenin's appetite disappeared. She had always been a glutton, but now she just looked at her food dish. Old age, we thought. She also began sleeping in unexpected places, just outside the bathroom door, for instance. Twice I found her wandering off to strange corners where she'd never been. She looked confused, as though she didn't know what she was doing. Kitty dementia, we joked.

Less than a week after her loss of appetite, she started looking sick, listless and glassy-eyed, and we took her to the vet. Tests showed no obvious cause of illness, and the vet wondered if she could have been poisoned. Neither of our two younger, more inquisitive cats had been sick so poisoning seemed doubtful. We left her at the vet overnight, where she would be placed on an IV for nutrients and hydration.

One of our other cats had gotten sick one time, and a couple of days on an IV had helped her kick whatever virus she'd picked up. Surely Thevenin would recover, we thought. An affectionate peacemaker who had always tried to soothe us when we were angry or upset, she had earned the right to die quietly in her sleep.

When we visited Thevenin the next day her appearance shocked us. She was unconscious, and when she finally stirred she didn't recognize us. We took her home, foolishly hoping she would get better if we just gave her lots of attention. At the very least Thevenin would get to die in her basket.

After we got home, I lay down with Thevenin stretched out on my chest. She had always rumbled like a motorboat when she was petted, but she just lay there, a dead weight. One time she lifted her head to look at me, but I doubt if she recognized me. After about an hour she began to move restlessly.

I carried Thevenin to her basket. She struggled weakly to stand up, and she couldn't. Instead she flopped around, twitching, while her bowels voided, then lapsed back into unconsciousness. We rushed her back to the vet for a fast, painless death.

Afterward we brought her body back home and buried her in the rose garden. A concrete block in the shape of a peace sign marks her grave. I just wish she had spent her last night at home and had been put to sleep while she could still recognize us.
—Sandra Williams
http://www.WilliamsWriting.com

If you are upset and distressed, your cat will sense it and may also become agitated. We do not know if they understand why you are not calm. Gently stroke your cat's head and provide comfort and reassurance.

Your cat may sense her time has come and that you are there to help, as usual. As far as we know, cats do not get upset at the prospect of their own death. Sadness and regret are human, not feline, feelings.

If you stay with your cat during the procedure, it will not be easy. Expect to cry. Once the procedure is over, you will probably feel a sense of completion. Now you can return home to clean up the evidence of the past few days or weeks of animal care.

On the other hand, if you do not wish to be present, you can drop the cat off at the vet. If you can't stand the thought of watching your cat die or are repelled by the sight of needles, hand the cat over to the vet.

Many cats dislike riding in the car because they connect cars with getting stuck with a needle. If your cat dislikes the vet's office, ask the doctor about a house call.

If you pay in advance, you will be able to give your full attention to your cat and avoid the risk of crying while writing a check in the waiting room.

This time it vanished quite slowly, beginning with the end of the tail, and ending with the grin, which remained some time after the rest of it had gone.
—Lewis Carroll (1820-1914)
Alice's Adventures in Wonderland.

Beams of Light

It came on the cold, gray, rainy first day of spring in 1991. Nick had spent the previous day and a half in the closet. We knew it was time. I held Nick while the doctor injected him. I felt the last beat of his heart.

I held him a moment longer, then we left the vet's office, grateful for the rain that masked our tears. We were only a mile or so from the ocean, so we went to stand near the surf and collect our thoughts.

We hadn't been there more than 5 minutes when the thick, gray clouds over the ocean parted and beams of light sprayed from the heavens to the ocean surface. It was Nick, saying thanks.

—Robert Goodman, San Diego.
rg@SilverCat.com

Body positions. Rigormortis, a temporary stiffness of muscles occurring after death, will occur in a few minutes. Whether the cat dies naturally or is euthanized, you may wish to lay the cat in a circular "sleeping" position and close her eyes in preparation for burial. When the face muscles relax and gravity takes over, the lips may pull back into a grimace. This is natural and not due to pain.

Disposing of the body. Unless your cat died of a contagious disease such as rabies, you are free to bury it, cremate it or leave it with the vet for incineration. Or, you may wish to "keep" the cat through taxidermy, freeze drying or cloning. The decision may depend on yard access, local laws and how much you wish to spend.

✔ **Burial**. If you bury your cat in your yard or a friend's yard, the grave should be at least three feet (1m) deep to discourage scavengers. Place the cat in a shroud of cloth and lay him or her in the bottom of the hole. Lay a board or wire screening on top in case a scavenger should dig that deep, and fill up the hole with dirt.

Bury the cat as soon as possible after death; it will begin to decompose quickly.

Blondie
We had the funeral immediately. We simply laid Blondie in the grave wrapped in her towel. We put an orange rose on her and said our good-bye. Each one of us put some dirt on her; my husband planted an azalea bush above her head and filled the hole. Our prayers were silent.

We spend the rest of the night talking about her, what she meant to us, how we felt. The whole event had been very sad and heart wrenching, but at the same time it was also full of grace and love. As a family we felt very close and bonded in our loss.
—Beate Fisher
omsairam@bellsouth.net

If you bury your cat in your yard, you may erect a headstone. You may wish to plant flowers or a bush to mark the grave.

London
London was 17 when she died in my arms. She was diagnosed
with kidney failure in December of '96, and lived until January
of '99. Neither of us would give up. Her half sister, Bridget,
was 18 when we "put her to sleep" in May 2000.

Neither way of losing such a loved family member is easy. I
live in Minnesota and January is not a good time to try and
bury a cat. We cut trees at the farm and tended a fire for a
couple of days to soften the ground for digging. We buried her
out on the point overlooking the river. Bridget joined her last
spring. It is a beautiful, quiet place to sit and remember our
sweet kitties.
—Dorothy Molstad, Minnesota.
Dendoor@aol.com

If you select burial and do not have a back yard or
your municipality prohibits pet burial except in
designated locations, consider a pet cemetery. You
may schedule a ceremony, drop off the cat at the
cemetery or a pickup service may be available. See
"Pet Cemeteries" in the *Yellow Pages*.

Message in a Bottle
We didn't ask about city regulations when our cats died.
Instead, we bury them here at home. I write up the data (name,
age, date of death) and put the slip of paper in a small bottle
and we bury that with our departed cat friend.

Catnip grows on their graves, out under the lilacs and
honeysuckle. Small stone or concrete markers locate the graves.
When the snow is gone and the leaves and grass aren't out yet,
I can see them.
—Pat Bell, Eden Prairie, Minnesota.
http://www.catspawpress.com/

☑ **Cremation.** Many people today choose cremation. Then you have the choice of scattering kitty's ashes in her favorite places or bringing them home in a jar. See the listings under "Pet Cemeteries & Crematories" in the *Yellow Pages.* They may also have a memorial garden for pet ashes.

We cremate all our animals, even the horses. I have all of them at home on shelves. Cremation is better than burial as there is no risk of bulldozing or other disturbance.
—Leo Grillo, Acton, California.
D.E.L.T.A. Rescue

☑ **Incineration.** Your vet can dispose of the body for you. The remains will be collected for cremation by a firm licensed to incinerate animal remains and other "medical waste."

☑ **Taxidermy.** Some cat guardians have their cat "stuffed" although the results are often disappointing. Only the skin, fur and claws will be real. The eyes will be glass and the facial expression will be frozen and may appear distorted. Ask to see samples of the taxidermist's work. See the Yellow Pages for local taxidermists. You may opt for placing a more-accurate photograph on your mantle.

☑ **Freeze Drying** removes water from the cat's body and takes about six months. It is similar to mummification.

Cloning hit the headlines in 1997 when Scottish scientists at Britain's Roslin Institute successfully cloned Dolly from an adult sheep cell. The possibilities excited cat guardians who desired to duplicate a departed pet.

In cloning, a small skin sample is taken and grown in a laboratory. The nuclei is extracted and inserted into a recently ovulated egg cell. Then the cell is implanted in a surrogate mother cat. If all goes as planned, the surrogate mother will give birth to a kitten genetically identical to the original donor cat.

Animals are products of both heredity and environment. Cloning duplicates the tissue donor, the genetic parent. The clone will have the same sex and genes, both good and undesirable. But the experience of growing up will not be the same for the new cat. Your cat clone may  look the same and have the same general temperament but is unlikely to act the same. The cloned cat will have her own personality. Personality and behavior are mostly the result of experience and education, rather than genes. You may be disappointed that the cloned cat does not act like the original—and resent her.

Cloning is not perfected. Some 30 percent of cloned animals are abnormal.

A cell taken from a cat knows how old it is. If the donor cat is 12 years old, the cells in the kitten will think they are 12 years old. Older cells do not copy themselves as efficiently, so the clone is likely to age faster.

Some people are banking tissue samples from their cats waiting for the day when cloning is more reliable and the price for cloning becomes reasonable.

Cloning is a new and quickly evolving science. For the latest information, make a search on the Internet and see
http://www.messybeast.com/clonecat.htm

Coping with your loss. Grieving is normal and should not be suppressed. Many people go through the four stages of grieving: denial, anger, depression and acceptance. Many of those around you will be unable to understand what you are going through. You may wish to share your loss with others who have had the same experience recently. See
http://www.animalmedical-dental.com/html/book/grieving.htm

See rec.pets.cats, alt.animals.felines or the many bulletin boards and forums on the Net. See the appendix and About.com.

See Moira Allen's advice at
http://www.pet-loss.net/surviving.html

Effect of the death on the family. A child and a cat enjoy a special, bonded relationship. The cat is a reliable playmate, bedmate and companion. The child feels needed and appreciated with unconditional, non-judgmental love. So, when the cat dies, the child often takes it very hard.

Animals are such agreeable friends, they ask no questions, they pass no criticisms.
—George Elliot (1819-1880)
She was an English Victorian novelist.

Fibbing to your child that the cat has been "sent to the country to live happily on a farm with other kitties" robs that child of the education and understanding of the difficult concept of death. Do not take from your child this important learning experience that will help him or her to cope with larger loses in the future.

Assess your child's feelings by asking whether he or she wants to perform a funeral or burial service. Involve your child in the decision-making process. Children appreciate being included, having situations explained; they like straightforward, truthful and simple answers. If they are involved and work through the decision-making process with you, they may be better prepared to accept the pet's death.

Experts advise against telling your young son or daughter that the cat is "being put to sleep" as the child may expect the animal to wake up and return. If you euthanize the cat, your child may be confused and think the vet's office is where animals are killed just as some think fire trucks *bring* fires. Or, your child might be afraid to go to sleep for fear of not waking up.

Death is a learning, and growing, experience. Involve your child in the decision if old enough. It is likely that your child will learn the truth someday— probably after figuring out Santa Claus, the Easter Bunny, and the Tooth Fairy. Your child won't resent you for fibbing on these three. See http://www.griefnet.org/KIDSAID/dougypage.html

Effect of the death on the other pets. No one can say what cats know or feel but there are countless stories of cats inspecting a dead house-mate and reacting in very human ways. Of course,  the remaining animals will adjust their territory and hierarchy but we do not know for sure if they mourn.

Snuffy

For more than five years I had been feeding a gray feral cat I call Gray Kitty and allowing him to spend the Minnesota winters in my garage. This cat never allowed me to pet him, always ran away when I came with food, but in time did become tame enough to sit on the porch with my other two cats.

When Snuffy was dying, I took my gasping cat out on the porch about 4 AM hoping he would be able to breath the damp night air more easily. I was sitting there holding him on my lap when the feral cat crawled out from under the porch and took his usual position sitting there, keeping my ailing cat company.

I left Snuffy on the porch in the feral cat's company, thinking my own cat might be dead by the time I woke in the morning. He wasn't.

Snuffy moved from spot to spot in my yard as he tried to find a position that might enable him to breathe more easily. The feral cat followed him and kept him company wherever he went, sitting respectfully a few feet away from him.

I went out every half hour or so to check on Snuffy, always having to look for where he was hiding.

About 9:30 AM I noticed the feral cat back on my porch, and knew then that my cat had died.

I never found my cat's body, but know he crawled under a porch or into a thicket to die. I also know the gray cat was deliberately keeping him company in his last hours. It was an amazing thing and still brings tears to my eyes.
—Diane Haugen, Barnesville, Minnesota.
http://www.wcdd.com/index.html

As long as there is no danger of infection, it may help any other surviving animals to inspect the body. It is possible that they understand death and accept it as an explanation for their missing playmate.

When an animal is dying, we bring its close friends to visit. At home, our other pets come by and make their own peace with the deceased—sort of a wake—before we remove him for cremation.
—Leo Grillo, Acton, California.
D.E.L.T.A. Rescue

Memorializing your cat. Focus on the good times. Remember the happiness and pleasure you gave to each other.

Here are some ways others have honored their departed cat.

✔ Tombstone or plaque. Place an engraved marker in your garden even if you did not bury your cat there.

✔ Hold a special service with your family.

✔ Visit some of the places you shared.

✔ Plant a tree, yourself or through a service. See http://www.treegivers.com/program.html

✔ Write a poem. Post it on your bulletin board, refrigerator or Web site.

✔ Keep a journal of your feelings as you pass through each stage of grieving.

✔ Write down your memories. Create a written tribute.

✔ Make a donation in your pet's name to a cause that you believe in. A local animal shelter may have a memorial wall where you can place an engraved plaque.

✔ Take out an ad in the obituary section of your local paper.

✔ Post a tribute on your own Web site or on a pet-loss site.

✔ Write a letter to your departed cat and read it often.

✔ Attend pet bereavement support groups, live or online.

✔ Visit an animal shelter to see other cats but do not adopt—yet.

✔ Purchase a special urn for the ashes if you had your cat cremated.

✔ Frame a photo of your cat and place it in a place you will see often. Or have a portrait painted from the photo.

✔ Put the photos of your cat in a scrapbook.

See http://www.rainbowbridge.com/
See http://www.petmemories.com/home.html

Rainbow Bridge

Anonymous

Just this side of Heaven is a place called Rainbow Bridge. When an animal dies, that has been especially close to someone here, that pet goes to Rainbow Bridge. There are meadows and hills for all our special friends so they can run and play together. There is plenty of food, water and sunshine, and our friends are warm and comfortable.

All the animals who had been ill or old are restored to health and vigor; those who were hurt or maimed are made whole and strong again, just as we remember them in our dreams of days gone by. The animals are happy and content, except for one small thing; they each miss someone very special to them who had to be left behind. They all run and play together, but the day comes when one suddenly stops and looks into the distance. His bright eyes are intent; his eager body quivers. Suddenly he begins to run from the group, flying over the green grass, his legs carrying him faster and faster.

You have been spotted, and when you and your special friend finally meet, you cling to each other in joyous reunion, never to be parted again. The happy kisses rain upon your face; your hands again caress the beloved head and you look once more into the trusting eyes of your pet, so long gone from your life but never absent from your heart.

Then you cross Rainbow Bridge together........

The Animal's Eden

The Animal's Eden is a huge, beautiful walled garden where all pets go until such time as their human companions can join them. Only pet animals go to this walled garden and there are other special places for all the other animals, and  especially beautiful places for animals who have suffered while on Earth and whose souls need peace and healing before they can move on. The garden is full of lawns and hedges, flower borders and shrubberies, wildflower meadows and patios of red brick. All of this is surrounded by a wall, just like a Middle Ages English garden, but much, much larger. The wall is not to keep the animals in and the garden is so huge that none of them feel as though they are in any way enclosed. And in any case there is a special gate, but I will come to that later.

In the Animal's Eden all the pets that have passed over and are waiting for their special human, are free to do what they want, and because it is a heavenly place, none of them want to do anything that harms their animal friends. The horses and ponies graze and gallop in the meadows. The dogs romp on the lawns and sniff in the shrubberies. The cats lounge on the patios, basking in the sunshine, or take their ease in the dappled shade of trees. Birds are no longer caged, but fly free in the trees, eating the plentiful fruit and seeds. None of them actually feels hungry, but are provided with heavenly food if they wish so that they can eat without harming the others waiting alongside them. The garden is full of every kind of animal that has ever been a pet and has someone special it wishes to wait for.

There is a special arch in the garden wall, the sort of brick arch that might have held a wrought iron gate in earthly gardens. Sometimes one or more of the animals gets a funny feeling, a bit like butterflies in the tummy. Those animals stop their playing or basking and make their way to the arched gate. Something special is about to happen. When they reach the gate they can see that their special human is walking towards the gate. Then, because the Animals' Eden is a place for animals only, those animals can walk through the arch to join their human friend(s) and walk together in the sunshine on the next stage of their souls' journey. For although the garden is a beautiful and happy place, there is nothing more joyful than a reunion between dear friends who have been apart too long.

The Animal's Eden was written by Sarah Hartwell. She has relinquished her copyright and released it to the public domain so that it may be freely distributed. http://www.MessyBeast.com

🐈🐈🐈🐈🐈🐈🐈🐈🐈🐈🐈🐈🐈🐈🐈🐈🐈🐈🐈🐈

Benefits of sharing your home with a cat. In the U.S., 12 people out of every 100 over age 15 live alone, including nearly a third of those who are 65 or older, 41 percent of women age 65 and older, and more than half of women age 75 and over. More than half of all women will be widowed or divorced by age 65.

Studies show that people who share their homes with pets have less stress in their lives and live 3 percent longer. A cat provides the opportunity to care for and nurture another living being who will return unconditional love. Cats are great house-  mates; they are independent, take care of themselves, love to cuddle and are great listeners.

Should you adopt another cat? You can never replace the cat you lost but you can get another to share your life. This will be a new cat, not a replacement cat. While the new cat may resemble the previous cat, their personalities will be different. Purebreds will differ and mixed breeds will differ even more. Understanding this, some people prefer to avoid confusion by remembering the previous cat as he was and to get a new one that looks entirely different. Then they can concentrate on the new housemate rather than being uncomfortably reminded of the former pet.

I have recently gotten a new cat friend—from a no-kill shelter. Her name is Daisy and she, on purpose, doesn't look like either of my deceased cats.
—Dorothy Molstad, Minnesota.
Dendoor@aol.com

If the previous cat was poisoned, abducted, eaten by predators such as coyotes, or run over in the street, you may decide it is unwise to put a new cat at risk in your neighborhood.

Or, perhaps you are getting along in years and realize that a kitten may outlive you. Perhaps adopting an older cat makes sense.

If you have other pets in the house, they may or may not readily accept an intruder. Most will get used to each other, establish a pecking order and re-divide territory over time. Some will become fast friends. Make sure that all have been vaccinated and do not pose a health risk to each other.

When should you get a new cat? Some people adopt a new cat immediately while others need a period of grieving before they are ready to give their love to a new cat. There are no rules and both approaches are normal. The death of a pet may be emotionally upsetting. Make sure you are over your grief before taking on the responsibility of a new cat. Premature replacement may cause a personal conflict.

Your cat died at his chosen time to "make room" for his brother who is waiting for you. Do not let your cat die in vain—he pushed over. Adopt now.
—Leo Grillo, Acton, California.
D.E.L.T.A. Rescue

If your cat died of an infectious disease, ask your vet how long it will take for any bacteria left in the house and yard to die; it may take 3 to 30 days. Some people will accelerate the cleanup with disinfectants while others limit the use of toxic chemicals in their home.

Where should you get a new cat depends on whether you want a pedigree or non-pedigree pet.

✔ **If you want a pedigree cat**, check ads in cat magazines and visit exhibits at cat shows. Also consult pedigree rescue societies. Purebred cats lose their homes too and while these cats are usually older and may have lost their papers, you can get a loving purebred cat.

Be very careful of other sources such as ads in the local paper, many pet shops, swap meets and super-market bulletin boards. Fly-by-night cat vendors and kitty mills are only interested in turning a quick sale. The kitten may be sick, not vaccinated or poorly socialized. These cats often come with counterfeit papers and are unregisterable. Better sources for purebreds are reputable breeders, animal shelters and vet clinics.

✔ **To adopt a non-pedigree cat,** see your local animal shelter and ask your vet about cats and kittens needing homes. Many vets take in stray and abandoned cats and turn them over to a shelter. And vets have many clients with healthy newborn kittens.

Afterword

You are going through a difficult time and have many important decisions to make. When I found myself in your position, I shopped for a book but could not find one.

Cricket was over twenty when he began to decline. As an author, I work at home. Cricket and I did everything together and were companions 24/7.

I played nurse and took care of him for his last three weeks as I desperately searched for more information. This is the book I wish I had read to help me with Cricket's decline.

Dan Poynter

Appendix

Resources

Books

On Cat Health

The Country Vet's Home Remedies for Cats by David Kay. Publications International, 1998.

Cat Owner's Home Veterinary Handbook by Delbert Carlson & James Giffin. Hungry Minds, 1995.

Natural Health Care for Your Cat by Dr. Rudolf Deiser. Barron's 1996.

Natural Healing for Dogs and Cats by Diane Stein. The Crossing Press, 1993.

Doctors Book of Home Remedies for Dogs and Cats by Matthew Hoffman. Rodale Press

Natural Pet Care by Gary Null, Ph.D. Seven Stories Press, 2001.

Illustrated Veterinary Guide by Chris Pinney. McGraw-Hill, 2000.

Merck Veterinary Manual. Merck & Co, 1998.

Authors like cats because they are such quiet, lovable, wise creatures, and cats like authors for the same reasons.
—Robertson Davies (1913-1995) Canadian novelist and playwright.

Veterinarian's Guide to Natural Remedies for Cats by Martin Zucker. Three Rivers Press, 2000.

Why is Cancer Killing Our Pets?: How You Can Protect and Treat Your Animal Companion by Deborah Straw & Gary Kowalski Inner Traditions International, Ltd., 2000.

Bach Flower Remedies for Animals by Helen Graham & Gregory Vlamis. Findhorn Press, 1999.
http://www.FindhorPress.com

The New Natural Cat by Anitra Frazier. EP Dutton, 1990.

Dr. Pitcairn's Complete Guide to Natural Health for Dogs and Cats by Richard H. Pitcairn. Rodale Press, 1995.

Natural Cat Care: A Complete Guide to Holistic Health Care for Cats by Celeste Yarnell, Book Sales, 2000.

On Life Extension

Caring for Your Older Cat by Chris C. Pinney
Barron's, 1996
The Ultrafit Older Cat by Claire Bessant & Bradley Viner. Smith Gryphon Ltd, 1993. Available from http://www.Amazon.co.uk

Defy Aging by Michael Brickey, PhD.
(For humans)
http://www.NewResourcesPress.com

On Dying

Preparing for the Loss of Your Pet: Saying Goodbye with Love, Dignity, and Peace of Mind by Myrna M. Milani. Prima Publishing, 1998.

Surviving the Heartbreak of Choosing Death for Your Pet by Linda Mary Peterson. Greentree Publishers, 1997.

Palliative Care in the Home by Derek Doyle. Oxford University Press, 2000.

Final Gifts: Understanding the Special Awareness, Needs, and Communications of the Dying by Maggie Callanan. Bantam Books, 1997.

The Art of Dying: How to Leave The World with Dignity and Grace, at Peace with Yourself and Your Loved Ones by Patricia Weenolsen & Bernie Siegel. St. Martin's Press, 1997.

On Pet Loss

For Every Cat an Angel by Christine Davis. A very nice giftbook for the grieving. Lighthearted Press, 2001. http://www.lightheartedpress.com/

Pet Loss: A Thoughtful Guide for Adults & Children by Herbert Nieburg, Arlene Fischer & Martin Kosins. Harper Perennial Library, 1996.

Coping with Sorrow on the Loss of Your Pet by Moira. Anderson, M. Ed. Alpine Publications, 1996. http://www.pet-loss.net/emotions.html

Coping with the Loss of a Pet by C.M. Lemieux. Wallace R, Clark, 1988.

Absent Friend by Laura & Martyn Lee. Trafalgar Square, 2000, Ltd. 1992.

Goodbye my Friend by Mary & Herb Montgomery. Montgomery Press, 1991.

The Loss of a Pet: New Revised and Expanded Edition by Wallace Sife. Hungry Minds, 1998.

The Final Farewell: Preparing for and Mourning the Loss of Your Pet by Marty Tousley & Katherine Heuerman. Our Pals Publishing, 1997.

Goodbye, Friend: Healing Wisdom for Anyone Who Has Ever Lost a Pet by Gary Kowalski. Stillpoint Publishers, 1997.

Crossing the Rubicon: Celebrating the Human-Animal Bond in Life and Death by Julie Kaufman. Xenophon Publications, 1999.

Three Cats, Two Dogs: One Journey Through Multiple Pet Loss by David Congalton. Newsage Press, 2000.

Cold Noses At the Pearly Gates: A Book of Hope by Gary Kurz, 1997.

Loving and Losing a Pet: A Psychologist and a Veterinarian Share Their Wisdom by Drs. Michael Stern and Susan Cropper. Jason Aronson, 1998.

The Legend of Rainbow Bridge by William Britton. Savannah Publishing, 1994.

Good-bye, Dear Friend by Virginia Ironside. Robson Books, 1996.

Between Pet and People by Alan Beck and Aaron Katcher. Purdue University Press, 1996.

When Your Pet Dies by Christine Adamec. iUniverse.com, 2000.

Friends for Life: Loving and Losing Your Animal Companion by Carolyn Butler, Suzanne Hetts and Laurel Lagoni. Two audiocassettes. Sounds True, 1997.

Death to Dust by Kenneth V. Iserson, MD, What happens to dead bodies (human). Galen Press, 2001. http://www.galenpress.com/

It's Okay to Cry by Maria Luz Quintana, Shari L. Veleba & Harley King. K&K Communications, 2000.

Books for Children

Talking About Death: A Dialog Between Parent and Child written by Earl S. Grollman and illustrated by Susan Avishai. Beacon Press, 1991.

The Tenth Best Thing About Barney by Judith Viorst. Aladdin Books, MacMillan Publishing Co., 1999. Ages 5 and up.

The Accident by Carol Carrick. Houghton Mifflin, 1981. Ages 4-8.

Bristle Face by Zachary Ball. Holiday House, 1991. Ages 9-12.

The Yearling by Marjorie Rawlings. Aladdin, 1988.

*Will I see Fido in Heaven?
Scripturally Revealing God's
Eternal Plan for his Lesser
Creatures* by Mary Buddemeyer-
Porter. Eden Publications, 1995.

*Mr. Rogers' First Experience:
When a Pet Dies.* Paper Star,
1988. Ages 4-8.

My Pet Died by Rachel Biale.
Tricycle Press, 1996.

*A Special Place for Charlee: A
Child's Companion Through Pet
Loss* by Debby Morehead &
Karen Cannon. Partners In
Publishing, 1996.
Grade level 3-6.

Cat Heaven by Cynthia Rylant.
Scholastic Trade, 1997. Ages 4-8.

**Veterinarians, Animal Care
Professionals, and Health
Care Professionals**

*The Practical Guide to Client
Grief* by Laurel Lagoni.. AAHA
Press, 1997.

*Pet Loss and Human Emotion:
Guiding Clients Through Grief* by
Cheri Ross and Jane Baron-
Sorenson. Accelerated
Development, 1998.

Associations & Institutions

The Association for Pet Loss and
Bereavement.
http://www.APLB.org

American Association of Feline
Practitioners.
http://www.aafponline.org/

The American Veterinary
Medical Association.
http://www.avma.org

Animal Welfare Information
Center, USDA
http://www.nal.usda.gov/awic/ind
ex.html

American Animal Hospital
Association
http://www.aahanet.org/

American Board of Veterinary
Practitioners
http://www.psln.com/medhead/ab
vp.html

Associations for Complementary
and Alternative Veterinary
Medicine
http://www.altvetmed.com/associ
at.html

American Veterinary
Chiropractic Association
AmVetChiro@aol.com

International Veterinary
Acupuncture Society
http://www.ivas.org/members1.ht
m

International Association for
Veterinary Homeopathy

http://www.altvetmed.com/iavh.h
tml

National Center for Homeopathy
http://homeopathic.org

Nelson Bach, USA, Ltd.
http://www.nelsonbach.com/index
2.html

Cat Fanciers' Association
http://www.cfainc.org/

Center for Thanatology
(study of dying).
http://www.thanatology.org/

Magazines & Newsletters

Animal People
Merritt Clifton & Kim Bartlett
anmlpepl@whidbey.com
http://www.AnimalPeopleNews.o
rg

Fanc-e-Mews ezine
http://www.cfainc.org/ezine/index
.html

Cat Fancy Magazine
3 Burroughs
Irvine, CA 92618-2804

Medical Insurance

Cats United Services
http://www.catsunited.com/html/c
at_insurance.html

Veterinary Pet Insurance.
http://www.petinsurance.com/affi
liates/planet-
pets/default.cfm?&js=1

Chat Rooms, Listservs

and Newsgroups

alt.support.grief.pet-loss

Rec.Pets.Cats
http://www.fanciers.com/cat-
faqs/index.html

alt.animals.felines

Cats, General

MessyBeast.com
Cat Resource Archive.
http://www.messybeast.com/
jshartwell@aol.com

Blakkatz Cattery
http://www.blakkatz.com

Feline Future diet
http://www.felinefuture.com

Feline www sites
http://felinewww.com/

NetVet and the e-Zoo.
http://NetVet.wustl.edu

Animal Medical and Dental
Center
http://www.animalmedical-
dental.com/siteindex.htm

Cat Stuff
http://victoria.tc.ca/~wy236/Catst
uff.html

21 Cats.org
For detailed advice on most cat
diseases, see
http://www.21cats.org/health.htm
l#0

Veterinary/Medical Information
and Veterinarians
http://www.pibburns.com/catvet.
htm

"Virtual" Veterinary Center -
Martindale's Health Science
Guide
http://www-
sci.lib.uci.edu/HSG/Vet.html#DI
CTION

MediPatch Laboratories. All
natural products.
http://www.holisticfamilyandpets
.com/

PetMed Express.com
http://www.PetMedExpress.com

Foster & Smith catalog
http://www.DrsFosterSmith.com

Foster & Smith Pet Education
site
http://www.PetEducation.com

Pet Food Institute
http://www.PetFoodInstitute.org

Cat Fanciers Resources List
http://www.fanciers.com/lists.htm
l

http://www.CatsPrayer.com

Cat Aging

Purina Senior Cat Center
http://www.catchow.com/senior_T
OC.asp

http://www.OlderCat.com

http://www.AgingCat.com

http://www.AgeingCat.com

http://www.CatGerontology.com

http://www.FelineGerontology.co
m

Cat Dying

The National Hospice and
Palliative Care Organization
http://www.nhpco.org/

Painlaw.org. Legal resources on
palliative care and pain
management.
http://painlaw.org/palliativecare.
html

http://www.DyingCat.com

http://www.DecliningCat.com

http://www.CatThanatology.com

http://www.FelineThanatology.co
m

http://www.CatEuthanasia.com

http://www.FelineEuthanasia.co
m

Cat Loss/Bereavement

Moira Allen's
Pet Loss Support Page
http://www.pet-loss.net/

The Pet Loss Grief Support
Website
http://www.petloss.com/

http://www.CatLoss.com

Pet Bereavement
http://www.catpractice.com/berea
ve.html

Cat Memorial

Cat loss sympathy cards
http://www.fortunecity.com/mille
nium/rainbow/339/plcards.html

The Virtual Pet Cemetery
http://www.mycemetery.com/my/
pet_menu.html

Final Plans
http://www.nvo.com/finalplans

Rainbows Bridge.com
http://www.rainbowbridge.com/

In Memory of Pets
http://www.in-memory-of-
pets.com/

Pet Bereavement Resources

The Animal Medical Center, New
York
212-838-8100

PetFriends, Inc., NJ
800-404-7387

St. Hubert's Animal Welfare
Center, NJ
973-377-7094, Tuesday evenings

ASPCA-New York
http://www.aspca.org/nyr/death.h
tml

Pet Loss & Grieving
www.cowpoke.com/Pages/Pethom
e.htm

Estate Planning
http://trfn.clpgh.org/animalfriend
s/genlink2.html

Cat loss Counseling Centers and Hot Lines

The University of California-
Davis, Veterinary School of
Medicine
www.vetnet.ucdavis.edu/petloss/i
ndex.htm
916-752-4200

Cornell University Feline Health
Center
607-253-3414
www.vet.cornell.edu/public/petlos
s

University of Florida
352-392-4700 (Then dial 1 and
then 4080)

Iowa State Pet Loss Group
http://www.vetmed.iastate.edu/su
pport

Chicago Veterinary Medical
Association
630-603-3994

Tufts University School of
Veterinary Medicine
508-839-7966

Michigan State University
517-432-2696

Ohio State University
614-292-1823

Virginia-Maryland Regional
College of Veterinary Medicine
540-231-8038

The Grief Recovery Institute
Beverly Hills, CA
888-773-2683

Chicago Veterinary Medical
Association
Chicago, IL
708-603-3994

Michigan State University School
of Veterinary Medicine
Lansing, MI
517-432-2696

The University of Illinois
http://net.cvm.uiuc.edu/CARE/

University of Minnesota School of
Veterinary Medicine
Minneapolis, MN
612-624-4747

Pet Friends
Morristown, NJ
800-404-7387

Lightning Strike
http://www.lightning-
strike.com/frame_pet-loss.htm

The Pet Therapy Society of
Northern Alberta
http://paws.shopalberta.com/PTR
emember.htm

The Rainbow Passage,
Pet Loss Support and
Bereavement Center
Grafton, WI
414-376-0340

Software

Catz. A virtual cat alternative.
Catz® are virtual Petz™ that live
on your computer desktop. From
little kitty-Catz, you raise them
as they grow, play, and learn
together. When they grow up,
many will start families of their
own. Can be ordered from the
site and sent as a gift. $19.95
http://www.petz.com/

Index

Colophon

This book was completely produced using the New Model production system described in *Writing Nonfiction.* See http://ParaPublishing.com

Research and gathering
Web: MS Explorer 5.0
Encyclopedia Britannica online
Art: http://www.ArtToday.com

Writing and manuscript building
Manuscript preparation: MS-Word 2000
Typefaces:
Body text: New Century Schoolbook, 12 pt.
Headers: Arial, 12 pt.
Chapter titles/subtitles: New Century Schoolbook, 18 pt. Bold.
Chapter numbers: New Century Schoolbook, 18 pt. Bold, Italic.
Quotations: Arial, 11 pt. Bold.
Stories: Garamond, 12 pt.
Appendix: New Century Schoolbook, 9 pt.

Cover design: Robert Howard Graphic Design

Conversion
MS-Word to PDF: Adobe Acrobat 5.0

Printing
McNaughton & Gunn, Saline, Michigan.

Paper: 60# white offset book.
Cover: 10 pt C1S, four-color, layflat film lamination.
Binding: Perfect bound (adhesive, softcover)

OlderCat.com

Where cat guardians go for answers

Quick Order Form

⬛ **email orders:** orders@ParaPublishing.com.
🖺 **Fax orders:** 805-968-1379. Send this form.
☎ **Telephone orders:** Call 1(800) PARAPUB toll free (727-2782). Have your credit card ready.
▣ **Postal orders:** Para Publishing, Dan Poynter, PO Box 8206-146, Santa Barbara, CA 93118-8206. USA. Telephone: 805-968-7277

Please send the following Books, Discs or Reports. I understand that I may return any of them for a full refund—for any reason, no questions asked.

_____

_____

_____

Please send more FREE information on:
☐ Other books, ☐ Speaking/Seminars, ☐ Mailing lists, ☐ Consulting

Name:_____

Address:_____

City _____State _____Zip: _____-____

Telephone: _____

email address: _____

Sales tax: Please add 7.5% for products shipped to California addresses.

Shipping by air:
US: $4 for the first book or disk and $2 for each additional product.
International: $9 for 1st book or disk; $5 for each additional product (estimate).

Payment: ☐ Cheque, ☐ Credit card:
☐ Visa, ☐ MasterCard, ☐ Optima, ☐ AMEX, ☐ Discover

Card number: _____

Name on card: _____Exp. date: ____/____

See http://ParaPublishing.com